MW01234979

GOD
ANGELS
DEMONS

CAL POULSEN

ISBN 978-1-0980-3854-0 (paperback)
ISBN 978-1-0980-3855-7 (hardcover)
ISBN 978-1-0980-3856-4 (digital)

Christian Faith Publishing, Inc.
832 Park Avenue
Meadville, PA 16335
www.christianfaithpublishing.com

Printed in the United States of America

CONTENTS

INTRODUCTION

I have written this book to tell a story of God's intersessions in our lives. From the time we were children to aging adults, God has never ceased to work with us. I ask you to look into your past and recognize the wondrous times that God has intervened in your life. Whether it was God protecting you or somewhere you may have entertained an angel, maybe he came to your rescue during a vivid dream or a physical encounter of some kind. Whatever the case, God was there for you.

This book depicts eight narratives of stories associated with God and his angels. The final four narratives tell a different story. They are about Satan and how he can take over your dreams. They are about Satan's abilities, both physically and spiritually, and how he can occupy this physical world one minute then attack you spiritually the next. He doesn't want to scare you. He wants to physically eliminate you or at least maim you so a part of your body sustains physical damage. This has all happened to me.

I have tried telling my story to other believers, including some pastors. Their support for me was shallow at best. This book is for you so you will know that there is someone out there who understands what you have gone or are going through. My prayers are with you!

PERSONAL HISTORY
OF CAL POULSEN

- Christ believer for thirty-six years

- Church administration

- Youth director, administration

- Church finance

- Music director

- IHSA-certified referee, basketball

- Focused Bible study group leader

- Biblical relationship counseling

- Deacon

- Lay Pastor, training

- Army veteran, three years (1967–1970)

SECTION 1

How It All Started

In October 2012 I was invited to participate in a men's Saturday morning Bible study starting at 7:00 a.m. This was a little difficult in the beginning. By the time it ended at 9:00 a.m. I found that I was finally fully awake. At this time there were thirty-four members, a generous cross section of talents and personalities, but they were leaderless like a ship without a rudder. They were in the process of watching a video dedicated to tithing. I do not remember who the speaker was, but it focused on what is known as the *prosperity gospel* found by *prooftexting* various scriptures from the Bible, combining them and calling them fact.

> *Prooftexting* (sometimes *proof-texting* or *proof texting*) is the practice of using isolated, out-of-context quotations from a document to establish a proposition in eisegesis (introducing one's own presup-

positions, agendas, or biases). (Wikipedia) https://wikipedia.org/wiki/prooftext

Prosperity theology...is a controversial religious belief among some Protestant Christians, who hold that financial blessing and physical well-being are always the will of God for them, and that faith, positive speech, and donations to religious causes will increase one's material wealth. (Wikipedia) https://wikipedia.org/wiki/ Pray for money

The capstone of this subject came as an admonishment from God himself is this:

Will a man rob God? Yet ye have robbed me. But ye say, Wherein have we robbed thee? In tithes and offerings. (Mal. 3:8)

This scripture was written to the nation of Israel (Jews) over four hundred years before the New Testament. Nowhere in the Bible are the Gentiles (you and me)—the Body of Christ—directed to tithe. The Jews during the time of Jesus were still under the Law and therefore were required to tithe. In most cases the tithe (tenth) was turned over to the Levitical priests. Today we are free to give financial donations of any incremental size to the church.

When the video was finished, you could hear the buzzing and chattering of many of the group members as they pared off in twos and threes. They were obviously discussing what they had seen and heard over the last hour. Not being able to hear what was being said, I waited for order to be restored. Finally, after several minutes went by, the video's leader regained control. After he asked if there were any questions, a major argument ensued that lasted throughout the whole final hour. In this chaos, I decided to sit this one out.

What you need to understand is that tithing or not tithing has never been a requirement for salvation. You can't buy your way into heaven. Over the next three weeks, I was actively participating in the various discussions. I found myself in complete disagreement with almost every subject that came up. I very carefully brought the group's attention around to the fact that we should be studying Christ, his crucifixion, shed blood, burial, resurrection, and ascension unto the Father forty days later. This is what we need to study while accepting God's free gift of grace. Jesus tells us that his grace is sufficient for us. For "by grace are ye saved…" (Eph.2:8–9) Grace allows us to look into the scriptural time capsule of the apostle Paul and how God chose him to lead the Body of Christ.

> For by grace are ye saved through faith; and that not of yourselves: *it is* the gift of God. (Eph. 2:8; italics added)

> But unto every one of us is given grace according to the measure of the gift of Christ. (Eph. 4:7)

> For the grace of God that bringeth salvation hath appeared [Jesus] to all men. (Titus 2:11)

This turn of events did not go well. It actually fractured the group. A little over half wanted to study the facets on how to follow the Law—why we should be baptized and give account for our reasoning or give our testimony and that the Gospels of Matthew, Mark, Luke, and John are the keys to salvation. If this is true, then they who believe these are proselytes, for the Gospels were written for the Jews. Proselytes are Gentiles who have committed themselves to the Jewish faith. Some have gone so far as to believe that they and the church today are the spiritual Israel. Nothing could be farther from the truth. Little did I know of the impact this study would have on me.

Several weeks later, the one group split into two groups. It turned out that fourteen of the men wanted to follow Christ. It was then that I was asked to become the "spokesman" for the group and its teachings. We prayed together, and we stayed together for six years and eight months, covering 119 biblical topics. I printed over thirty-eight thousand pages of written testimony and spent thousands of hours in research, comparisons, and analysis. None of it was work. I felt blessed that God had given me this opportunity to share his beloved Gospel of salvation through the apostle Paul.

> Moreover, brethren, I [Paul] declare unto you the gospel which I preached unto you, which also ye have received, and wherein ye stand;
>
> By which also ye are saved, if ye keep in memory what I [Paul] preached unto you, unless ye have believed in vain.

For I delivered unto you first of all that which I also received, how that Christ died for our sins according to the scriptures;

And that he was buried, and that he rose again the third day according to the scriptures. (1 Cor. 15:1–4)

Companion verses

"But what saith it? The word is nigh thee, *even* in thy mouth, and in thy heart: that is, the word of faith, which we preach;

That if thou shalt confess with thy mouth the Lord Jesus, and shalt believe in thine heart that God hath raised him from the dead, thou shalt be saved.

For with the heart man believeth unto righteousness; and with the mouth confession is made unto salvation.

For the scripture saith, Whosoever believeth on him shall not be ashamed" (Rom. 10:8–11; italics added).

The following scriptural account was prepared in July 2019 for a local pastor who was having trouble understanding "the age of grace" and the differences between Christ crucified and the Gospels of Matthew, Mark, Luke, and John.

It is also a fact that at this time the apostles had no idea what Christ was going to go through. They did not understand that he must die and shed his blood. The shedding of his blood brought in the beginning of the New Testament of truth and salvation based upon his death and resurrection. Scripture itself tells us that this fact of his shed blood was kept from them.

> And they understood none of these things: and this saying was hid from them, neither knew they the things which were spoken. (Luke 18:34)

This is also the message that I started sharing in 2015. I am sure that the message of Christ's shed blood caused the five physical (spiritual) attacks that I suffered. It was obvious that Satan had to do something to silence me. His attacks, as written in Section 6, did not work and never will. Although those attacks were painful physically, mentally, emotionally, and spiritually, God protected me and gave me the strength to endure. I hope that you find this compilation interesting and informative. Your life will depend on it.

Thursday was the day I reserved for my final preparation for the coming Saturday's 7:00 a.m. to 9:00 a.m. Bible study. It was a blessed time. Hours of prayer and preparation finally came together in a form that could be shared with others. I thought about high-fiving myself, but then I thought, *What's the point?* So I gave God a spiritual high five. I am sure he appreciated it in some fashion.

That day should have been no different. I was thoroughly excited about sharing 1 Corinthians 15:1–4 that the apostle Paul called "the gospel" of salvation. I had prefaced this discussion the week before with a ten-minute introduction. All I saw were twelve smiling faces that were elated to finally get to the New Testament understanding of Christ's shed blood. The men wanted more information than I was willing to give out. I reassured them that there is a time and a place for everything. This was the place but not the time. With a slight bit of laughter over my pun, we all agreed and noticed that it was 9:05 a.m. It was time to go home.

As we continued our journey the following week, I found that it was necessary to share the trials and tragedies that Job and his family went through. Then we would proceed into 1 Corinthians 15:1–4.

Job's Story

We all know that Satan can physically harm us or even cause death, yet he needs God's permission to do so.

> And the Lord said unto Satan, Behold, he
> *is* in thine hand; but save his [Job] life.
> (Job 2:6; italics added)

You may have studied the story of Job, an upright man in God's eyes and faithful in all things. God blessed everything that Job and his seven sons and three daughters did. They were wealthy beyond measure. Satan could not influence Job because God had a hedge put around him, and all he had were from God and his holy angels. Let's look at the story of Job and its impact on him through the eyes of the New International Version Bible. The story covers Job 1:1–22.

In the land of Uz there lived a man whose name was Job. This man was blameless and upright; he feared God and shunned evil. He had seven sons and three daughters, and he owned seven thousand sheep, three thousand camels, five hundred yoke of oxen and five hundred donkeys, and had a large number of servants. He was the greatest man among all the people of the East.

His sons used to hold feasts in their homes on their birthdays, and they would invite their three sisters to eat and drink with them. When a period of feasting had run its course, Job would make arrangements for them to be purified. Early in the morning he would sacrifice a burnt offering for each of them, thinking, "Perhaps my children have sinned and cursed God in their hearts." This was Job's regular custom.

One day the angels came to present themselves before the Lord, and Satan also came with them. The Lord said to Satan, "Where have you come from?"

Satan answered the Lord, "From roaming throughout the earth, going back and forth on it."

Then the Lord said to Satan, "Have you considered my servant Job? There is no one on earth like him; he is blameless and upright, a man who fears God and shuns evil."

"Does Job fear God for nothing?" Satan replied. "Have you not put a hedge around him and his household and everything he has? You have blessed the work of his hands, so that his flocks and herds are spread throughout the land. But now stretch out your hand and strike everything he has, and he will surely curse you to your face."

The Lord said to Satan, "Very well, then, everything he has is in your power, but on the man, himself do not lay a finger" [italics added].

Then Satan went out from the presence of the Lord.

One day when Job's sons and daughters were feasting and drinking wine at the oldest brother's house, a messenger came to Job and said, "The oxen were plowing and the donkeys were grazing nearby, and the Sabeans attacked and made off with them. They put the servants to the sword, and I am the only one who has escaped to tell you!"

While he was still speaking, another messenger came and said, "The fire of God fell from the heavens and burned up the sheep and the servants, and I am the only one who has escaped to tell you!"

While he was still speaking, another messenger came and said, "The Chaldeans formed three raiding parties and swept down on your camels and made off with them. They put the servants to the sword, and I am the only one who has escaped to tell you!"

While he was still speaking, yet another messenger came and said, "Your sons and daughters were feasting and drinking wine at the oldest brother's house, when suddenly a mighty wind swept in from the desert and struck the four corners of the house. It collapsed on them and they are dead, and I am the only one who has escaped to tell you!"

At this, Job got up and tore his robe and shaved his head. Then he fell to the ground in worship and said:

"Naked I came from my mother's womb,

and naked I will depart.

The Lord gave and the Lord has taken away;

may the name of the Lord be praised."

In all this, Job did not sin by charging God with wrongdoing [italics added].

Satan is relentless. He has physical power over the elements and people who did not honor God. Even after what he did to Job through his family, Satan still wanted more. Satan was determined to prove that Job would curse God under the right circumstances. Satan wanted to attack Job. Let's follow this part of the second story in Job 2:1–10.

> On *another* [italics added] day the angels came to present themselves before the Lord, and Satan also came with them to present himself before him. And the Lord said to Satan, "Where have you come from?"
>
> Satan answered the Lord, "From roaming throughout the earth, going back and forth on it."
>
> Then the Lord said to Satan, "Have you considered my servant Job? There is no one on earth like him; he is blameless and upright, a man who fears God and shuns evil. And he still maintains his integrity, though you incited me [God] against him to ruin him without any reason."

"Skin for skin!" Satan replied. "A man will give all he has for his own life. But now stretch out your hand and strike his flesh and bones, and he will surely curse you to your face."

The Lord said to Satan, "Very well, then, he is in your hands; but you must spare his life" [italics added].

So, Satan went out from the presence of the Lord and afflicted Job with painful sores from the soles of his feet to the crown of his head. Then Job took a piece of broken pottery and scraped himself with it as he sat among the ashes.

His wife said to him, "Are you still maintaining your integrity? Curse God and die!"

He [Job] replied, "You are talking like a foolish woman. Shall we accept good from God, and not trouble?"

In all this, Job did not sin in what he said.

As we can see, Job went through some tremendous trials. Although physically successful, the point is that Satan failed in everything he did against Job. It is important to note that Satan needed permission from God before he could do anything. Yet God, in his wisdom, would not allow Satan to take the life of Job. All these scriptural facts and all these stories do not give an account on what Satan can do when we are sleeping. Satan and his demons do not sleep. There is no timeout for Satan. Like thunder is to lightning, Satan and his demons also work through the night.

SECTION 2

God's Protection

Chapter 1

The Rat

July 1957, Racine, Wisconsin

There was no school, it was summertime with beautiful sunny days, and best of all, I was ten years old and ready to play my heart out. For me, living in farm country was the best of all worlds. Open fields, grasslands, planted fields, and plenty of wooded areas provided the backdrop for a day of exploration and fun. Most backyards were usually boring, but not ours.

For really hot days, we had the traditional swing set that was well-used and a little creaky. But our backyard was kind of special. There was room to play ball, plenty of trees to climb, and the best place was the abandoned chicken coup at the back right-hand corner of the property. Missing the door and all its windows and with its rotted and tattered siding gave it the appearance of being haunted. The wood flooring was mostly rotten, but even with these conditions it was a great place to play army. The standard order of the day from our parents was, "Stay out of the chicken coup." We always had the bad habit of taking our parents' directions as grown-up suggestions. But why not? With five kids in the family and Dad at work, it was hard for Mom to keep track of all of us.

All families in the country had a dog. We were not the exception. Our canine beauty was an eighty-pound pure-bred female German Shepherd named Tash. She was a great family dog—obedient, poised, and always ready to accompany us outside. She was fun, and she provided excitement when playing fetch. Like all shepherds, she was dedicated to the family, providing security and safety at all times.

The only drawback Tash had was when we were playing outside. If we began to run, she would assess the situation and for some reason decided that running was not safe. She would launch herself in the runner's direction, and when catching up to them, she would gently nip at his or her heels. Tash would keep this up until the runner stopped running. Then she would take off after the next victim.

However, today was going to be special. Agreeing with the neighbor boys the night before to play army, we wanted to get out early to prepare our rubber-band guns. These guns were made from a two-by-four that was two-feet long, with the rubber bands made from old inner tubes. Cutting the tubes into approximately one-inch-wide strips supplied us with the ammunition we needed for the day.

Before we could get outside, a huge tractor with a large, rusty bucket at the front came rumbling down our gravel driveway. The driver's intentions were unknown. Watching from inside the house, we decided that the best place to be was outside. Bounding out the back door, we positioned ourselves alongside the swing set while watching the tractor driver lower its bucket to the base of the dilapidated chicken coup. Black diesel smoke belched from the tractor's exhaust, and with the engine whine increasing the tractor began to inch its way forward until the bucket bumped against the coup.

Even at ten years old I knew that our beloved chicken coup was destined to be torn down. The thought had barely materialized in my head when the whine from the tractor increased to a deafening level. Slowly letting out the clutch, the old coup resisted its fate of demolition. It creaked, groaned, and crackled but didn't give in. The tractor whine increased even more with copious amounts of black smoke streaming into the air. For a moment I thought I saw a beleaguered frown pass across the face of the tractor's driver. Unimpeded, he let the clutch out all the way. The tractor bucked up and down like a horse rejecting its saddle, and then with the crackling of splintering wood the coup gave way. It literally exploded off of the wood foundation it was sitting on. It slingshot itself about two feet into the air and landed about three feet away from its original position. The tractor, now unimpeded, effortlessly pushed the old coup off of its foundation in a maze of pieces.

After several passes, the tractor had scooped the old coup off of the foundation into a pile, looking somewhat like a crumpled wooden pyramid with the roof's peak at its center. However, the rotted wooden floor remained in its original position. Looking quite satisfied at his work, the tractor driver backed up turned around and proceeded back down the gravel driveway. Turning left onto the paved asphalt road, in just minutes he was just a dot on the horizon.

Looking at the pile of carnage that had been the old chicken coup, none of us were sure what to do. A little curious, we all walked over to the wreckage to inspect it using the rotted wood floor of the coup as a shortcut. Walking over the floor while inspecting for upturned nails, I noticed some movement off to my left next to the wooden flooring where the entry door used to be.

Some dirt and wood pieces had been scraped away, exposing what looked like a small tunnel about the diameter of a soda bottle. I stooped down to inspect my new find just above the entrance to the hole. Looking down, I was surprised to see about six to seven baby mice curled up just inside the entrance. I thought, *Now we are talking exploration.* Since I had never seen a mouse before, I thought they looked kind of cute. But then mischief set in.

What should I do with the mice? Before I even thought about it, I had the ultimate solution: take each mouse and put them all down a gopher hole. Boy, would that be a surprise to the gopher. Taking one by the tail, I stood up. Dangling by its tail, it wiggled and jiggled like a worm on a hook. I raced over to the nearest gopher hole and placed the mouse inside the entrance. Looking right at home, down the hole it went. I raced back to get another. I picked a second one up by the tail, then I raced over to a second gopher hole. Down it went. I couldn't help but laugh to myself while wondering what the gophers thought.

Going back for a third mouse, I bent down to pick one up. About three inches from my hand was the biggest mouse I had ever seen! It must have come out to see what all the commotion was about. About this time, all of the kids were watching me stuff mice down the gopher holes and had watched my return. This time, a little fun was about to be turned into a tragedy. From head to tail, this grayish-brown mouse/barn rat was about eighteen inches long, with its lips curled back and baring its teeth, it made the most horrible screeching sound.

I instantly stood up and began to run toward the back door of the house. My feet and legs were churning as fast as they would go, but I felt as if I was running in slow motion. I just couldn't seem to gain any speed. To be safe, I knew I had to make it to the back door and into the safety of the house before the rat got to me. As far as I was concerned, the other kids were on their own. Too afraid to turn around, I just kept my legs going, with arms pumping out a rhythm to match my feet. For what seemed like an eternity, I ran past the swing set, still heading for the back door. Just twenty more feet, and safety. For some reason, my hearing kicked in, sensitized to the screams of the other kids: "Run! Run!"

It was obvious that they knew more than I did or I even wanted to know. I was just two steps from the door when I came skidding to a halt, with dust and small stones flying. I unceremoniously crashed into the back door, grabbed the handle, and turned around. What I saw and happened next was all in slow motion. Turning around, I was at eyeball height with the rat. It had leaped toward me, suspended in the air, with feet and claws stretched out. It was within six inches of landing onto my face. At that same instant, I saw a blurry shape and movement to my left. Instantly, I was now focused on the biggest teeth and snarling sound I had ever heard! It was our German Shepherd, Tash! She was in midair with an open mouth, teeth lashing out at the converging rat. In that same instant Tash bit down on the rat, stopping its forward momentum. As she, with the rat in her mouth, flew past me, I felt her soft fur brushing past my face.

Landing on all fours with the rat in her mouth, Tash shook her head fiercely before finally dropping the dead rat at my feet. Tash sniffed the dead corpse several times and then looked up at me. Her eyes told me that she was concerned for my safety. As I leaned over to pet her, she rubbed her body against my legs, showing the ultimate affection.

Chapter 2

Ford Falcon

September 1966, Lake Geneva, Wisconsin

I was in my raven-black mag-wheeled Ford Falcon with 4-speed on the floor. With its 265-horsepower engine, this was my baby, as I gently accelerated and decelerated because of the winding and hilly road conditions. I was returning to Racine, Wisconsin, from a day of fishing in Lake Geneva.

It was always a fun drive on Highway 50, east-bound at a speed limit of sixty-five mile per hour. It was late afternoon when I breezed along on a long, steep, downward-sloping hill. No cars came, and none were behind me. There was, however, a car sitting—stopped—at the bottom of the hill in a small valley-like impression in the oncoming lane at a noncontrolled intersection.

As I approached the car, it still did not move to turn left or continue going straight. It just sat there. I actually paid little attention to it after that. Still cruising at approximately sixty-five, I entered the bottom of the hill's intersection and came to within about fifty feet from the stopped vehicle when it suddenly started turning left, crossing into my lane directly in front of me. I could see the woman in the passenger seat screaming, mouth open, looking at me with her hands pressed against the window glass of the passenger-side window.

The only thing I remember after that was a loud thud, the screech of tires on pavement, and my car coming to a standstill in the middle of my lane approximately one hundred feet past the car that was turning left. As I looked in the rearview mirror, the car was just completing its turn and then came to a stop. I remember shutting off the engine of my car, taking my foot off of the brake, and opening the car door.

At the radius point of the intersection behind my car, there were twin-tire skid marks that looked as if it came from the left-side tires of my car. The skid marks were on the right side of the oncoming traffic lane. At that moment, I finally realized that I did not broadside the other car.

The other people were out of their car, walking over to me and asking if I was alright. Intermittently, the woman was shouting expletives toward who I assumed was her husband. Moving to the front of my car, I assumed that there was a major amount of damage to the front end and grill assembly. To my surprise, there was very little damage to my car—just a slight wrinkle to the right front fender just above the right-side front tire. Reviewing the damage to the other car, I found none that was apparent—just a couple of scratches of the right rear outside radius of the car's steel bumper.

After exchanging driver and insurance information, we both went our ways. I remember taking a mental note of congratulating myself for my defensive driving capabilities yet wondering how any of us were still alive after such a close encounter. Was I that good? Or was I just that lucky? Starting my car, depressing the clutch, shifting into first gear, and being just a little overcautious, I checked for any opposing traffic at the front and rear and slowly accelerated back onto the highway for the trip home, distancing myself from those two black skid marks.

Chapter 3

The Antenna

June 1978, Racine, Wisconsin

It was in the early evening in mid-June while watching TV that I decided that the current program I was watching on WTMJ-TV Milwaukee was of no interest anymore. Besides, the picture was a little fuzzy around the edges. This was due to the rooftop antenna. Although old, it was doing the best job it could on the limited signal strength available.

Changing channels to WGN Chicago, I dutifully activated the rotary antenna on my three-story brick home to the proper southeast direction. Just a turn of the wrist, and I would have a perfect picture on our twenty-four-inch console Motorola TV. The control box began its usual low growl as the dial rotated to the southeast position that I had set it to. The picture faded to a multicolored collage as the antenna sought out the new signal. Stopping precisely on "SE," I became a little concerned about the clarity of the picture since there wasn't one.

Toggling the rotation dial a little to left or right did no good. All I got was the low growl from the control box as it sought out the new direction. To my frustration, it became obvious that the dial, although rotating, had no effect on the gearbox mounted to the six-foot antenna pole that was mounted up on the twelve-foot tripod mount, which was anchored to the roof.

Something in the system decided to fail. So much for a relaxing evening in front of the TV. Not giving up, I carefully inspected the four-inch-diameter rotary directional dial with N-S-E-W marked on its face in white and the subsequent power connection at the back of the unit. I found nothing wrong. Not trusting my own senses, I decided to rotate the directional dial again, hoping for improved picture clarity. The directional control box emitted its customary low growl. The dial turned and stopped on the positional setting I had turned it to. The picture clarity did not improve.

With the limited use of cable TV in my area, the directional antenna was supposed to be "state of the art." Maybe that was the problem. I lived in "SE" Wisconsin, and WGN was in the "NE" corner of Illinois.

Having limited choices, I knew that my next move was laced with adventure and danger. There was no choice but to venture onto the steeply pitched roof, scale the tripod mast, reach the rotary gearbox, and begin my inspection of the unit—all of these at a height of fifty-five feet above good old terra firma and tied off to the top of the twelve-foot steel tripod with an overweight tool belt and no experience. Losing the early evening sunlight, I knew that this project was destined to begin tomorrow, Saturday, a day off.

The bright, sunny day began normal enough. Wanting to get a head start on the project, I got up early, ate a quick breakfast, downed a quick cup of coffee to ward off the usual midmorning caffeine headache, and then into the basement I went. It was tool time.

Finding my brown leather tool belt was easy enough. Topping it off with wire cutters, pliers, screwdrivers, several wrenches and, of course, a roll of black electrician's tape, I knew I had better get it right. I wasn't about to do the up-the-ladder-down-the ladder routine. Since I did a lot of tree cutting and trimming, I selected a half-inch-diameter, fifty-foot coil of rope to secure me in place once on the roof. Because of its severe pitch, I selected the stickiest soled pair of sneakers I had.

Exiting the basement door, I headed to the garage to get the aluminum extension ladder. Finding it, I headed to the north side of the house, planted the soleplates of the ladder firmly into the soft ground, and extended the ladder to its full vertical height. Leaning it against the house, I heard a high metallic clang as it came to rest. The ladder's top was resting on the gutter while protruding at about twelve inches above—not the best position to scale a ladder. This side of the house was my best option, not having the third exposed basement-level walkout. Shouldering the fifty-foot coil of rope, I began my ascent. As I climbed the ladder rung by rung, it had a tendency to bounce and sway left to the right just a little. It was just enough to make me rethink this strategy. Having no other alternative, I continued my climb. Reaching the gutter that was now at eye level, I grasped the protruding gutter with my right hand for security. At least the swaying of the ladder stopped.

Climbing two more rungs, my waist was now at roof level. Using my knees on the top rung of the ladder as an anchor point, I gently tossed the coil of rope up onto the pitched roof. As a passing thought, I now felt a lot safer with two hands freely grasping the top vertical sides of the ladder. Leaning forward from my perch on the ladder, I placed both hands palms down on the granular surface of the roofing shingles. Like a crab walking forward on all fours, I began the simultaneous upward movement of my feet and hands.

Now on the roof, I grabbed the coil of rope and briskly angled up the roof to the base of the tripod of the antenna. Grabbing the tripod base, I gave it a big hug while orienting myself to the panoramic setting I now found myself in. Slowly catching my breath, I uncoiled the rope and secured it around the base with the best gilligan hitch I had.

Paying out approximately twenty feet of rope, I secured it around my upper legs and waist, in case the worst should happen. Having come to an agreement with my perilous surroundings I stood up with my feet on the peak of the house and began the vertical climb up the tripod base, placing one foot after another on the base's horizontal bracket supports. This was easy-peasy. In just a few steps I reached the intersection point of the antenna pole and the tripod. Three feet above this point was my quarry the rotary gearbox. Two more steps up, and my face was directly across from the gearbox. Eyeing the gearbox with suspicion,

I immediately noticed that one of the low-voltage wires attached to the bottom input side of the box was broken.

To say the least, I was elated. Re-strip the wire's end, reattach it to the set screw, then tighten, and the job should be done.

As I was fastening the wire back into place, I heard the strangest sound. I listened intently; my hearing tuned to its optimum. Below me, at the base of the tripod, I heard what sounded like an acorn rolling down a shingled roof. The sound intensity diminished the further it rolled. After a few seconds I heard a tiny clunk into the bottom of the rain gutter near the ladder.

I froze in the ungainly position I had contorted myself into. My mind raced, trying to identify what could make such a sound. It took me a minute or so before I had the courage to look down at the three mounting bolts anchoring the tripod's feet that were anchored to a roof-mounted bracket.

Slowly turning my head and looking down, I saw that the two bolts anchored to one side of the roof bracket were in place. Slowly corkscrewing my head around, I looked down at the bolt-and-nut combination mounted to the last leg on the other side of the roof's pitch. Terror set in instantly. It was gone. It was what had rolled down the roof into the gutter.

At this thought and with my nervous wiggling on the tripod base, the one leg on the tripod base began to shake and clatter as if it was as fearful as I was. At that instant the whole assembly started swaying and then began to tip over, with the two bolted sides acting as hinges.

Instinctively, I leaned in the opposite direction, hoping that my weight would offset the disaster that was about to happen. It worked. The tripod assembly regained its upright vertical position. Momentarily staying off disaster, it felt like my heart was beating uncontrollably within my chest. Deep breathing helped, but for just a microsecond my mind glimpsed another bolt failing. Banishing that dreaded thought, I forced my mind to the reality of the task at hand. How was I to get off of this thing without dying or suffering from serious injury?

The only way down was the same way as I got up there. I found it easier to climb than to descend. Tool belt, a dangling rope, and a slight Southerly breeze, none would make my descent any easier. In my leaned position, I felt with the toe of my shoe for the closest lower horizontal tripod bracket. Finding it, I tested my weight on it, waiting for the mast to start tipping again. It didn't happen. It seemed as sturdy as ever. Taking a new handhold, I tried the other foot with success. Two more, and I could stand on the peak of the roof. Another handhold, and more success. Finally, the last step would set me free from this present danger. I had made it! But why was the tripod and mast so sturdy? Coming down the last couple of steps, I felt fully safe and secure. Standing on the peak, I decided to give the tripod a slight push. Immediately, it began tipping over.

I stopped its momentum and returned it to its upright position. At that moment, instead of feeling grateful, I felt as though I had tamed a beast. My ingenuity overpowered my senses by impressing upon me that it saved the day. I even wondered why I was so concerned about the danger involved in such a project.

Readjusting the rope and securing it to the chimney, I adjusted my gloves, walked to the opposite edge of the roof, and began rappelling down the three-story side of the house. I got as far as the bedroom windows when I heard a shrill terrified scream. It was my wife. She was just opening the window to holler up to me that lunch was ready. Instead, she sees me dangling just outside and below the window. I think her appreciation for me ebbed to an all-time low.

Yes, I did have to venture back up on the roof, but not for any repairs, except one. In the garage I found a one-half-inch bolt, washer, and nut to replace the one now lying in the gutter. The third leg was repaired; ropes were taken down; and tool belt, and ladder were put away. If you are wondering, yes, the rotary antenna was working once again. All of our favorite channels tuned in perfectly. There is one thing that I learned from this. If there is a next time, get cable!

Chapter 4

Potential Catastrophe

May 1979, Racine, Wisconsin

The early spring day dawned bright and cheery. Our almost two-year-old boy Michael was up and ready to be changed and fed. While Christi was seeing to his needs, I took a quick look in the diaper bag to see if it was well-stocked with all the essentials required for a needed visit to Christi's parents' home.

It included diapers, rubber pants, wipes, a change of clothes and, of course, a backup "binky." Since we had not seen them in a while, Grandma Dorothy and Grandpa Bill were excited to hear that we could make it on Sunday. Preparation for Christi and me was nothing unusual. A simple breakfast, coffee, toast for me, and cereal were all that were needed. By 10:00 a.m. we were ready for our adventure.

I began loading up the old Toyota 4-cylinder four-door grocery getter with the diaper bag and other miscellaneous stuff. It was one of those cars that comes along with your marriage. A good runner to a fault and also good on gas, I decided to start the engine and then waited. Christi emerged a short time later with Michael slung partially over her shoulder. He was giggling as usual.

Opening the passenger-side door, Christi ducked down with Michael to clear the overhead doorframe. Exchanging the typical pleasantries, I asked her if all was ready. Her answer came with the passenger-side door closing and a simple "Let's go see Grandma and Grandpa." With Michael on her lap and everyone as comfortable as they would get, we exited the driveway, turned left, and began our short journey. Even for a Sunday, the streets were more barren than usual.

Almost no cars were around. I found this to be quite elating compared to the usual Sunday morning church traffic. As we entered the downtown area, we came upon the usual stoplight every other block. Turning onto Villa Street where Grandma and Grandpa lived, we had to cross the three one-way lanes of 6th Street that was a major route to the interior downtown area. Then in just a short five blocks, we would be there.

We were in luck. The Villa 6th Street stoplight was green going in our direction, allowing us to drive through. As usual, I cautiously approached the intersection, checking for pedestrians and people on bicycles. Finding none, I began to accelerate through the intersection. I had not so much as nosed onto 6th Street attempting to cross the first of three lanes when a car approached at great speed, driving perpendicular to us, moving from our right to left. Running a red light, it was headed straight for the passenger side of our car. Flinching and ducking to the left, I waited for the impact. To my surprise there was no impact. Looking at the left-side rearview mirror, I just made out the rear of the car that ran the red light passing through the intersection. I also noticed that my light was still green. When my focus returned to normal, it took several minutes for my heart rate to return to normal. Christi was oblivious to what had just taken place. Knowing we were out of danger, I decided not to upset her by telling her what just happened. In reminiscing, I could just imagine all three of us being killed that day. Christi and Michael would have never stood a chance. For many years I have looked back at this incident, wondering why we were spared.

SECTION 3

God's Angels in My Life

Chapter 1

Elderly Woman (Chicago)

October 1980, Alabama transfer

4:00 a.m.—the clock's alarm jangled me out of what had been a good night's sleep. Can you even believe it? My nerves were not ready for this kind of disruption, especially this early on a Monday morning.

Diligently packing a week's worth of clothes, toiletries, and my favorite book the night before (Sunday) for a 6:30 a.m. flight from Chicago O'Hare International to Atlanta Hartsfield-Jackson International Airport was not my usual routine. I had to remind myself that this Monday morning, however early, was going to be very special. It was to be the first day on my new job as an engineering manager at a company in Eastern Alabama.

Now living in Racine, Wisconsin, this was going to be quite the job transfer. Forget about the culture shock from moving from the North to the South. I just wanted to make a good impression on the plant's employees and my new staff. I constantly reminded myself that very soon my family and I were going to become "Damn Yankees." Moving to the South and residing there was a big deal for us. There was possibly no snow and very little winter. Forget the fact that lunchtime would now be called dinner-time, and dinnertime was going to be called suppertime. Go figure. I thank the Lord that breakfast was still called breakfast. Either way, I didn't want to miss any of them.

I needed to hit the road by 4:30 a.m. for the one-and-a-half-hour trip from Racine to Chicago. After showering, dressing, and eating breakfast, I thanked my wife Christi for getting up at such an hour for me. Her pleasantries were a welcome break to my mind's repetitive thinking of the events that were ahead of me that day. Collecting my half-filled briefcase and verifying its contents, I shut the case. Grabbing the handle of a fifty-pound suitcase was more effort than I was almost able to muster. With a low grunt I was able to pick up the suitcase, kiss the wife goodbye, and head out the door. The thirty feet or so to get to my car was an effort in itself. Thankfully, at almost six feet two inches, I was tall enough that the suitcase cleared the concrete driveway by about one inch.

Opening the trunk of our 1979 Thunderbird Town Landau, with a laboring heave I swung the suitcase into the gargantuan trunk space common with that year's vehicle. Shutting the trunk, I opened the driver's side door and lightly slid across the gray leather seat. Placing the briefcase on the passenger-side seat, I keyed the ignition and started the car. As the engine came to life, I reversed the car and backed out of the driveway. Exiting to the street and all being clear, I pulled forward, clearing the curb and pulling onto the empty road. Turning left, I headed for Highway 20, a direct route to the I-94 toll road then east to Chicago. With the sun just peaking above the eastern horizon, dawn was slowly turning into day. Having traveled this route many times, I found the scenery quite boring. Turning the radio on, I listened intently to my favorite station, WLS.

Toll booth after toll booth, they all calmly digested the coins I dutifully tossed in the basket, obediently waiting for the green light to signal their success. This was becoming alarming. I was almost out of change. Finally seeing the O'Hare exit coming up, I cautiously shifted lanes all the way to the right and exited. Now on Highway 190 to the airport, I saw that my flight was originating in terminal 2. Driving over to the long-term parking area, I stopped at the gated entry and picked up my ticket. Fortunately, I found a parking spot just across the departure access road from Delta Airlines.

Muscling up to the occasion, I opened the trunk, grabbed the handle of the suitcase, and gave it the old heave-ho. Without losing any momentum, I reached up with my left hand; and placing my palm on the trunk lid, I closed the trunk to the pre-lock position. The auto-lock pulled the lid into place and secured it. I was now ready to go.

Slowly navigating the overhead pedestrian crossing, I entered the passenger terminal through the automatic doors, and with a hiss they opened at my presence. It was hard to miss the Delta counter. The wall behind the counter and baggage-weighing station had three-foot-high letters spelling out the airline's name. Below this, the baggage conveyor lay waiting for my suitcase. Depositing the suitcase on the weighing station and plopping my briefcase on the counter, I was welcomed with a cheery "Hello, and good morning!" from the ticket agent. Acknowledging her reception, I opened my briefcase and got out my driver's license and handed it to her. She found my reservation, tapped a few more keys, and then my airline ticket slowly appeared from within the printer. By then, my suitcase was weighed in at forty-eight pounds, and the baggage ticket proudly displayed ATL. Taking my plane ticket and license from the agent, I closed the briefcase and set out for the Delta concourse and the departure gate.

Pedestrian traffic was extremely light for a Monday. The time in the morning may have had something to do with that. About halfway to the gate, I was walking past a general seating area when I noticed that almost no one was sitting in the sea of chairs laid out before me. About twelve rows further along on the main aisle, I noticed an elderly woman slumped over in her chair.

As I approached her, I slowed my pace. Taking in the scene, I wasn't sure if I should check to make sure all was well or just keep on going. After all, this was Chicago. As I was making my way past her, she suddenly sat up in her chair, turned her head toward me, and stared directly into my eyes. Startling me, she had powder-blue eyes with a gray hue to them. Her silver-gray hair was neatly tied up in a bun and sat prominently on the crown of her head. Her weary thin face was expressionless. Except for the age lines etched in her skin around the outer portion of the eyes and mouth, she looked like there were many years of smiles associated with her age. She wore a black shawl around her shoulders, most likely comforting her against the slight chill that was in the air.

Before I could do anything, her lips began trembling slightly, and then orienting herself, she began to speak. "*For the change in your pocket, I will be able to eat today.*" Of all of the things I anticipated her saying, that was not on my list. Never answering her, I had the feeling I was being had, so I turned and continued my way down the concourse aisle. Looking back after a few steps, I noticed that she had her head down, looking at her lap. I picked up my pace, but my mind was reeling. The faster I walked, the more guilt I felt. Stopping in my tracks, I reached in my pants pocket and felt some small change and a folded dollar bill. I looked back, and she was still sitting there, as if frozen in time. Turning, I began walking back to her, having made up my mind to share what I had in my pocket.

As I stood in front of her, she looked at me. I asked her what she had said, knowing full well what the answer would be. "*For the change in your pocket, I will be able to eat today*." Digging into my right pants pocket, I cradled the dollar and change. Reaching out to her, she lifted her right hand up to me, palm open. Her hand was small and weathered. Fingernails slightly on the long side but nothing rakish, I placed my hand over hers and deposited the money I had. She said nothing. She just closed her hand around the money and placed her hand on her lap. Not knowing what to say, I turned and was again on my way.

I made that trip from Chicago to Atlanta about six times after that. I never saw her sitting in that chair again. The more I walked past that chair, the guiltier I felt. Later, I reasoned that giving, no matter to whom or for what circumstance, is the right thing to do. Temper it, yes. Do not be foolish. Show love and concern whenever the opportunity presents itself. I made the promise to God.

Note—the statement, "Thou shalt love thy neighbour as thyself," is found in Matthew, Mark, Romans, Galatians, and James. It is stated seven times in the New Testament— four times by Jesus, twice by Paul, and once by James. We are to help the weak and those who are in need.

Thou shalt love thy neighbour as thyself.
(Matt. 19:19)

We must help the weak, remembering the words the Lord Jesus himself said: "It is more blessed to give than to receive." (Acts 20:35, NIV)

Chapter 2

Milwaukee Ticket Counter (Tampa, Florida)

September 1993, airline blues in Tampa

Eight glorious days of spiritual and physical revival—the Feast of Tabernacles lasts seven days, followed by the eighth day or The Last Great Day. This is a Jewish holiday celebrated in late September or early October that is prompted by honoring God on the fifteenth day of Tishri, the first month of the year on the Jewish calendar. It is found in Leviticus 23:33–34.

> The Lord said to Moses, "Say to the Israelites: 'On the fifteenth day of the seventh month the Lord's Festival of Tabernacles begins, and it lasts for seven days.'"

Historically, the Feast of Tabernacles commemorates the forty-year period during which the children of Israel were wandering in the desert, living in temporary shelters. This is a major Jewish festival, having great religious significance. As a past member of Worldwide Church of God, the headquarters viewed the membership as an offspring of Judaism and called itself "spiritual Israel." Therefore, the connection between WWCG and the Jews was made.

The planning took place months before the actual trip did. Thousands of worshippers attended most of the major sites throughout the United States. Multiple meetings at members' homes, restaurants, and churches were the high point of every weekend that passed. Comradery exceeded friendships. Weekly sermons began intensifying the closer you would get to September. "Peanuts"[1] card parties were in vogue and where most of the major planning took place.

It was a great time for everyone. The year 1993 wasn't any different. Instructions came out for each of the feast sites; they were announced during a Sabbath sermon. You could see the excitement rising in all who were there. The edge of our seats was where we sat as information was given.

---

[1] "Peanuts" is a card game that relies on a combination of speed and patience. (It also has other names, such as Pounce, Nerts, and Squeal.) It involves players using their own personal deck of cards to create different piles of cards played in order while trying to get rid of all cards in one specific pile called the peanuts pile. It can be played by any number of multiple players but is best with two to four. (Ourpasttimes.com)

When could we call and make housing arrangements was the highlight of the sermon.

Imagine thousands of people sitting in their homes on a Sabbath (Saturday) evening after services looking at their phones, waiting for sundown so calls could be made. The hotel and motel businesses were so brisk that at times after dialing, all you could get was a busy signal. This was the Feast. This was like Christmas in July.

Truly, this year would be special. We were going to St. Petersburg, Florida, to the Bayfront Convention Center. Holding 8,600 people of like minds, singing special music, sermons, and children's activities, this was going to be very spectacular.

The appointed time came; and like a bird on a June bug, my wife Christi and her best friend, Judy, like kamikaze warriors, were on the scene and ready to go. Airplanes, rental cars, hotels—oh my! Can you get all of these done in one sitting? No matter the problems, they all turned into opportunities.

The day came, and it was time to leave for Milwaukee's Mitchel Field for our direct flight to Tampa/St. Petersburg, Florida. This would be the first time we had flown with friends to a Feast site. We were past excitement and rapidly converging on a perpetual form of euphoria. We checked our bags and got our plane tickets. The children were abuzz with kiddie chatter. Being an hour early, we had plenty of time to agree that, that evening the first dinner stop we would make in St. Petersburg was at The Brown Derby. Something about having a grog caught my attention as Judy tried to explain its ingredients—things like dark rum, lime juice, cinnamon stick, etc.—but I never heard what the last ingredients were because of everyone's raucous laughter.

She had gone on to explain that it was served in a glass the size of a washtub with a stem and needed two hands just to lift it. Forget about the taste; this baby was for show! Somehow, through all the laughter, we heard the PA system crackle. Several seconds later a female voice was heard explaining that we were now ready to board our flight. Noticing that we were about twenty minutes past our scheduled departure time, we were anxious to get going.

As our turn came to board the aircraft, a feeling of giddiness overcame everyone, except me. While standing in line, I observed our plane on the tarmac with a tad of disdain. This had to be the oldest working airplane in their inventory. I had an urge to go down and "kick the tires" as an element of self-satisfaction. If there was an older plane in their inventory, they were keeping it well-hidden. Down the gangway we went, all seven of us, except for our youngest daughter, Alissen. At the age of twelve she felt more comfortable skipping her way to the open door of the aircraft versus walking. A trademark of her age, I'm sure—not yet dignified but always ready for a good time.

As I handed my ticket to the flight attendant, I glanced to my right, looking down the aisle of the aircraft. I was convinced we had boarded a dinosaur with wings. Somehow, I couldn't convince myself that spending the next four hours aboard this beast was in my best interest. Finding our seats, I sat down and lightly buckled myself in. Small talk ensued with my wife, but I made sure my concerns stayed buried inside of me.

Time seemed to drag on. Ten minutes, twenty minutes, and we still had not pushed back from the gate. Finally, a flight attendant standing near the open cockpit door keyed her mic and began explaining that our aircraft was experiencing mechanical problems. A slight murmur emanated within the confines of the aircraft. Obviously, discussions were taking place between the passengers regarding the predicament we were in. With a soft grunt, a sheepish grin crossed my lips. My mind returned to the unrealistic thought I previously had about "kicking the tires" that would thereby guarantee the plane's readiness. With the age of this aircraft, I was feeling everything but confidence.

Within minutes a second flight attendant announced that the flight had been cancelled because of the previously stated mechanical problems, explaining that no replacement aircraft was available and that new bookings would have to be made.

The bulls' stampede began. People jumped up, entering the only aisle on the plane. They opened overhead compartment doors and began grabbing their stuff out of the overhead bins. This was a case of self-survival or survival of the quickest. The ensuing chaos had to resemble the exodus from Egypt. One thing that was lacking was leadership.

Taking matters into my own hands, I unclasped the seatbelt buckle cradled in my lap. Because of someone's backside virtually in my face, I was unable to stand up. Knowing how to fend for myself, I kicked into self-defense mode. I made sure that the backside in my face was not female; and recognizing that it wasn't, I contorted my body around to the left and, placing two hands on the small of his back, gave a mighty shove while standing up at the same time. Immediately, the top of my head encountered the edge of the overhead bin. Not knowing if blood was flowing, I glanced off the bin and continued to rise to my full six-foot-plus height. There! I made it. Feeling like the bologna in a meat sandwich, head throbbing, I grabbed my wife's hand and gave it a loving yank. The look I got was something like "REALLY?" I knew that she would thank me later.

Anchoring myself in the middle of the aisle, the sea of people behind me came to a halt. As my wife stood beside me, we slowly began moving forward toward the front of the plane. We were doing the itty-bitty baby two-step. Going nowhere fast, I resigned myself to the situation at hand. Finally entering the gangway, I felt like I could breathe again. After the aisle in the plane episode, the gangway looked like an unmarked four-lane highway. As we proceeded up the gangway, I couldn't help but wonder how we were going to get to Tampa/St. Petersburg, the final destination of our Feast Site.

Exiting the gangway, I was shocked to see four airline attendants waving their right arm like policemen directing traffic. The left was held out perpendicular to their bodies, pointing toward the direction they wanted us to go. The full impact of their gestures was about to become a horrible reality. They were herding us adjacent to the receptionist counter and positioning us into one long line. When I say long, I mean *long*. By the time we were positioned in line, there had to be over eighty people/families in front of us. Over the PA system, I could just make out a feminine voice telling us that they would re-ticket us on the first available flight to Tampa/St. Petersburg. This meant that they would book us to a later flight with the same airline. That older plane that they had in hiding came to mind.

Forget this! Huddling our group together, I had decided on a plan to circumvent this disaster. Being a frequent air traveler, I had earned my spurs on previous flight adventures. "This is what we are going to do! *Kids, listen up! You all stay here with Sherm (Judy's husband). Sherm, protect our place in line. Christi, Judy, and I will rush down to the main ticket counter for immediate service. Okay! Give me all of the boarding passes.*" With a slight nod, we were gone.

We walked as fast as we dared without causing too much attention. We didn't want the people who were now behind us in line to figure out what we were up to. A young couple was already headed in the same direction we were—down the concourse to, more than likely, the main ticketing area. Pointing to them, I implored my group to pick up the pace just slightly. It took a solid thirty seconds to pass them, but pass them up we did.

Reaching the main ticketing counter, I noticed that only two people from our doomed flight were already there talking to the ticket agent. Based on the amount of hand gestures I saw, it was actually a mini-argument. The two people talking to the agent were trying to get her to book them on a different air carrier. The last I heard was something about not being their policy. The agent then tried to influence us to return to our original gate.

My turn. I explained to the agent the importance of policies but that some policy decisions were not in everyone's best interests, and allowing us to book a different airline was akin to us "flying the friendly skies." Noticing my pun, she began to laugh. I then explained that the rest of our family—four children and one adult for a total of seven—were waiting in the torturous line at the gate, awaiting their fate. By now she had become my friend and agreed to book us on a competing airline.

After ten minutes of her fingers clicking on the keyboard, we finally had to settle for a flight from Milwaukee to Atlanta. No direct flights were available to Tampa. That was the first bad news. Remember that bad things or happenings come in cycles of threes. The second disappointment was that our arrival in Atlanta would be around 10:00 p.m., EDT. It was now 9:50 a.m. in the morning, CDT. Once in Atlanta, we had to connect with a flight to Tampa then rent our cars and…

It was now obvious that The Brown Derby and its infamous grog would have to wait for another time, place, and day. The party would have to wait. Instead, we found our way over to the new airline, checked in, and began our prison sentence at Milwaukee Mitchell Field Airport. We all new that this would be a day we would never forget.

Peanuts, soda, and the smell of leather—we were glad to finally be in the air. The soft, gray leather airline seats were a real welcome from the hard-backed chairs littering the waiting area in Milwaukee. It looked like our flight to Hartsfield-Jackson Atlanta Airport may not be so bad after all. Thinking ahead, I felt like I could take a little nap and get a little shut-eye. That was a fatheaded, wishful idea. I was sitting next to my twelve-year-old daughter, Alissen. Talking was one of her favorite pastimes. She had the window seat; I had the aisle seat. I thought the window seat would give her something to keep her busy—you know, count clouds or something. After all I should have known that there was nothing else to do at an altitude of twenty-eight thousand feet. Her nonstop chatter was sort of cute and funny for the first hour. After talking about every topic you could think of (except boys), the conversation turned to, "Dad, how long before we land?"

Except for my daughter's chatter, the flight was exactly what you would hope for—uneventful! As we began to descend, I was beyond tired. I didn't know how much longer we could keep going while keeping our eyes open. A brush with insanity crossed my mind, but I promised myself that I would be chipper until the very end.

Hearing the landing gear descend out of its hiding place and into the turbulent night sky was slightly deafening but refreshing. With a loud thump, it locked itself into place, ready for a night landing in Atlanta. I looked around and found that my daughter was now slightly turned to the right, looking out the window at the panorama of the city skyline. Words could not express the beauty of what she saw. Now was the time for looking, not for talking.

As the flaps were lowered, the sound of the rushing air outside the window became frenzied. Landing was only moments away. The craft waddled and swayed a little left, a little right, a little more power, a little less. The buildings that flashed by were the size of those found on a miniature train set yet getting larger by the second. We were about to land at the busiest airport in the world.

Concrete—that's all I could see. We were over the end of the airport runway. The jet engines were virtually silent as we floated over the tarmac. "Three, two, and one," I said to myself. With the screech of tires on concrete, we bounced, first down then up and down again. The nose of the aircraft slowly drifted into its aligned position, and we heard another small thud as its wheels touched down.

We heard a small clattering just as the brakes and reverse thrusters were applied. The roar of the thrusters was deafening—more like the sound of an out-of-control Niagara Falls. The plane shuddered and shook, throwing us slightly forward in our seats. The more the brakes were applied the more the plane shook. I couldn't help but think that this baby was going to need a brake job after this landing. In airplane speak, I was once told by a pilot that a landing was nothing more than a controlled crash. I really didn't need to know that.

Looking over at my daughter, her eyes were as big as saucers. I gave her a slight smile and a wink. She answered with a deep breath and an "I guess we made it." As we navigated down the taxiway, everyone began stretching and yawning. A female voice came over the PA system acknowledging that we, in fact, had just landed in Atlanta and thanked us for flying with them.

As the plane taxied to a stop, the electric-powered gangway was already moving into position to exit the passengers. A little fearful of what was going to happen when the seatbelt light was turned off, I braced myself for the worst. Was this going to be another free-for-all to latch onto our belongings, pillage the overhead bins, and make a sprinter start to exit the plane? With a ding-dong the seatbelt light flickered and went out. Surprising, even to myself I sat perfectly still, waiting for the mayhem that was about to begin.

Click, click, click, sounded from a few seatbelts being unlatched. Looking over the top of the seat toward the front of the plane, I noticed only a few people were standing in the aisle. They were like zombies. Moving stiffly, most of them looked like they had just gotten out of bed. Their hair was disheveled, and their clothes were wrinkled, giving an impression that the occupants had been in them for several days. Most were still yawning while some rubbed the back of their necks and eyes, and others were scratching a little here and a little there. It is amazing what people will do when they think no one else is looking. Smiling at this thought, I noticed my wife giving me the high sign that it was time to leave. Tilting my arm slightly toward my face, I quickly glanced at my Citizen diver's watch with the luminous dial. Self-generating and with no need for batteries or the sun, it was powered by daylight alone. It read 10:14 p.m.

Eyeing my daughter, I could tell that she was beyond ready to go. Retrieving our belongings, we waddled our way up the aisle and exited the plane for the laborious walk up the gangway. With great effort we reached the summit and turned left heading for the nearby ticket agent's counter. A small shot of adrenaline coursed through my body as I fully realized our dilemma. We were in Atlanta, not Tampa. Besides that, there was no one at the ticket counter.

Huddling our group together once again, I took a head count. All were present and accounted for. The accounted for was in the men's room taking care of business. Our plan was simple but strategic—hoof our way down to the main ticket counter and get the first flight to Tampa that we could get. The first step was getting out of this terminal area. I quickly checked the overhead signage for clues. There it was, the "Underground Train." This system was automated and ran underground. It was a people mover. This was the quickest way to transport ourselves to the maze of outbound ticket counters. "Follow the signs!" I hollered to nobody in particular. I wasn't worried about the children. They were like lemmings. As long as we were in the lead, they would blindly follow.

The signage led us to an escalator that descended forty feet into the inner workings of the airport. We were headed underground, yet as we descended the surroundings were cheery, well-lit, and for the travelers it was downright welcoming. The three CH-100 passenger cars were parked about one hundred feet off to our left, passenger doors open and inviting. There were three cars tethered together resembling a large segmented bug with articulated sections. Looking around me, I saw very few people with the same idea as we had. Heading for the lead car, our children insisted on sitting up front for the view. Disappointment was sure to set in once they realized we were in a well-crafted tunnel with nothing out there except the gleaming set of rails that would allow the passenger cars to find their new location near the ticketing area. Endless blackness seemed to stretch out before us with an occasional low-wattage light dotting the tunnel walls.

Settling onto our benches was welcoming to our aching bodies. As I was sitting, I barely heard the overhead synthetic voice say something, "This train is departing. Please stay away from the automatic doors." With a slight swishing sound, the double doors were closed with an audible thump. With that, the train jerked forward slightly and continued to pick up speed. The whine of the wheel-mounted electric motors continued to mount. Achieving maximum speed, we swayed slightly to the left and right, but by no means was the movement uncomfortable. An occasional high-pitched *clickity-clack, clickity-clack,* was heard as the steel wheels crossed a section of the glistening track.

According to the in-vehicle information display, we were finally approaching the domestic terminal ticketing area for Delta Airlines. This was a real-time intuitive video display. Several minutes later the synthetic voice came on again announcing our arrival and to stay clear of the automatic doors.

The doors opened with the accompanying whooshing sound of rushing air escaping into the terminal. Another head count ensued as we exited the train and entered the up escalator to ground level. It creaked and groaned, laboring intensely under the weight of the train's discharged passengers. As we exited the escalator to ground level, what we stepped into was mammoth in size. The tiled floors sparkled with the radiance of a late night with a full moon. Restaurants, bookstores, and kiosks were layered one next to another as far as the eye could see. The fast food chains numbered in the dozens with names I have never even heard of.

Pedestrians were everywhere. Some were running, some were walking and dragging baggage, and some just got in other people's way. Their equivalent energy to each of their individual situations was something to admire. Since I was almost running empty myself, I was slightly envious. Taking Alissen by the hand, I noticed that it was cold and slightly clammy. Looking up at me, she gave me a half frowny smile through a slightly pale face. Looking over to my wife, I was given a look that I fully understood.

Everyone's blood sugar level was running empty. As my mind grasped the significance of this reality, I knew that it was time to ingest large amounts of fast food with water and juice. In the meantime, I told my wife to haul the trail mix out of her haversack. Tearing open the bag with her teeth, she opened the large sixteen-ounce bag with ease. Like runners in a marathon, the bag was passed from person to person. Personally, I wanted to forgo the peanuts in favor of the M&M's and raisins. Respectfully waiting my turn, the half-empty bag finally made it over to me. Palming a small handful, I tossed them into my open mouth. It wasn't steak, but it was a whole lot better than the peanut-butter-and-jelly sandwiches that were purposely hidden in the bottom of the sack. With that solved, we moved on.

We desperately needed to find a flight departure information board. It was now coming up on 10:45 p.m., EDT. Finding one slightly off to my right, we angled in that direction. A small group of people's heads tilted skyward were reviewing the overhead posted information. Finding the Delta information was easy. The board was posted in alphabetical order.

Scanning the luminous board, I couldn't believe my eyes. The last posting in the column of information showed an 11:59 p.m. flight departure to Tampa from Terminal C out of Gate A21. Everyone was elated. Finding our way to the ticket counter, we noticed what should not have been.

After a day like we had, we found the counter lights out and no Delta agents on site. The computer monitors located at each station were like black holes emitting no illumination at all. The fact was we were in the right place. Disgruntled, our group headed over to the wall sitting area and sat down among about twenty other travelers. Huddling together with Judy, Sherm, and Christi, we discussed what our next option should be.

Nothing of any value came into our minds. We felt doomed. At a time when we should be filled with laughter and anticipation for the Feast of Tabernacles, we were instead filled with dread. Our plan was for Judy, Christi, and me to remain at the ticket counter while the others rested as much as possible. If we were lucky, we might be able to snag a Delta attendant who may walk by. Leaning on the ticket counter, we engaged in some small talk, but it didn't last too long. It was a hopeless effort in trying to be social. We spent most of our time there shifting our weight back and forth on our feet that were way past tired. Constantly scanning the corridor for a sign of help was, at this point, seemingly fruitless. We were worried that we would not be able to secure a flight to Tampa. Spending the night in the Atlanta airport was not one of our first selections. We should have been snuggled in our beds at the condominium while listening to the waves lightly lapping the white, sandy beach outside. A full moon was almost upon us. Reflecting the sun's rays, it looked like a round, white torch hanging by magic in the clear night sky. The stars, like glistening jewels, scattered throughout the heavens. Unfortunately, this was my imagination at work. Thinking about what we were missing was disheartening to me.

That thought came and went, as did many others. I perked up a bit when I saw a man about fifty years old approaching. To my chagrin, he was outfitted in blue maintenance uniform. With every step he took, a large set of keys was swaying and jangling from a belt loop at his left side. What looked like a name tag attached just above the left breast pocket was actually the name of the custodial service he must have worked for. "Colonial Custodial Services," it said.

His well-worn black shoes squeaked slightly on the glistening tile surface as he took each step. Within a few feet of us, he changed his direction and angled directly toward us. To our amazement, he carefully brushed past Judy and stood in the midst of the three of us. Being about five feet eight inches with curly, jet-black hair that was as short as he was, he had to look up to Judy to ask her, "Are you waiting for flight information?" His voice was soft yet straightforward as he made his inquiry. "Yes, we are," Judy replied, her voice rasping just slightly from a long day and lack of use. Without any hint of hesitation, he unclipped the keys from the belt loop and holding them up in his left hand began searching for a key with his right. After looking at them, it was evident that he was looking for just the right one. Finding it, he inserted it into the locked doorknob. Turning the key, we heard an audible click from the lock set. Turning his wrist to the right, the doorknob rotated, and the Dutch door opened with little effort.

As he stood at the Delta ticketing station, he turned to his right, grasped the nearest computer keyboard, and placed it on top of the counter. The monitor, being on a swivel base and already on the counter top, was easily turned to his line of sight. With one finger, he actuated the on button. The computer screen blinked once, then twice, and came to life, displaying a brilliant Delta logo. I was spellbound and in awe at what was taking place. Here, we had a maintenance man with keys to a restricted area activating a computer that allowed him entry into the private

Delta ticketing system. Nothing suspicious there. Looking at the expression on my wife's face, it was evident that she was silently cheering him on.

With a click he returned the keys to his belt loop. He then raised both hands, placing them just over the surface of the keyboard. Like a pianist at a concert, he began tapping the keys with an experienced, fluid motion. *Tap, tap, tap.* The screen changed. *Tap, tap, tap.* The Delta logo disappeared, and a new screen appeared. It said, "Enter Username," and below it, "Please Enter Password." Our goose was cooked. So much for elation, yet without a smidgeon of hesitation he began entering what we hoped was the correct username and password.

The screen went dark. We held our breaths. The screen came to life again displaying line after line of information. Simultaneously, we all exhaled. Taking in a new breath, we noticed that at the top center of the screen in the header were the words "Domestic Ticketing." With that, the man turned and asked what our names were. He entered all of the critical personal information that the computer system required. When prompted, he pressed the Enter key.

The computer posted our information to an 11:59 p.m. flight departure to Tampa from Terminal C out of

Gate A21. Asking if everything was correct, dumbfounded, none of us said a word. He then moused over to a large illuminated blue box that said, "PRINT." Actuating the Print button started a series of clicking noises that signaled a printer was hidden somewhere under the countertop; it had come to life. Performing its preprint checklist seemed to take forever. When the cycle was completed, the printer hummed, buzzed, and clacked out each of our tickets and boarding passes. Separating each ticket from its perforated edges was simple and quick. He turned around and handed us our boarding passes.

With that completed, he logged out of the program, turned off the computer monitor, and placed the keyboard back to its original place on the lower part of the counter. He rotated the monitor ninety degrees back to its original position. With that, he turned and closed the Dutch door behind him. With its self-locking feature the mechanism made a loud click as it slammed shut. Without saying a word, he turned and entered the tiled walkway, his black soled shoes squeaking as he went. As he left, Judy and Christi looked at me, and then they too turned to walk over to Sherm, giving him the good news. As they were leaving, I mouthed to them the words that I was going to follow him. By that time, he was about twenty feet in front of me. He walked to a pair of manual glass doors that exited to the outside. With little effort he opened the right-side door and passed through the opening. A few feet later he turned right into what turned out to be a pedestrian walkway. As I passed through the still-closing door, I also turned right. Getting my bearings, I found that he was nowhere in sight. Goosebumps the size of peas blossomed and protruded from my arms. The hairs on my arms were standing like forested trees in the wilderness. This can't be so! It's impossible! Yet still to my amazement, he was gone. This was not the first time this has happened. My mind raced back when several years earlier a man sitting on a bench with his chrome shopping cart outfitted with rubber wheels at a strip mall in Rockford, Illinois, had also disappeared.

Walking back to my family and friends seemed like it took forever. I must admit that I did turn around to look for him several times. As I reentered the ticketing area, I raised and outstretched my arms in a hopeless gesture of frustration. My whole family knew what had happened.

Epilogue

We finally boarded the L-1011 TriStar for our flight to Tampa. It turned out that the flight was quite full, and there were not enough seats in the center aisle to accommodate seven people. It turned out that the seat assigned to me by our maintenance friend was in an aisle seat next to a window. Since the window seat was empty, I decided to stretch out and relax on the flight to Tampa. I didn't think my wife was too happy with this arrangement but seemed to understand. Looking over to her, I blew her a kiss and waved night-night as I turned in my seat and closed my eyes.

Several seconds later, I was tapped on the shoulder. A young lady with a generous smile was asking if I would rearrange myself so she could take her seat by the window. Being an accommodating person, I exited my seat, almost hitting the overhead bin with my head. After all, being over six-feet-one-inch tall, this was quite easily done if you didn't look where you were going. Glancing over at my wife, if looks could kill, I would at least be wounded. Didn't she understand that this was not my fault? It was the maintenance man's fault. I found it very emotionally painful for me to reseat myself next to this young lady. I found myself reflecting on Proverbs 21:19 (KJV):

> *It is* [italics added] better to dwell in the
> wilderness, than with a contentious and
> an angry woman.

Knowing this, I got out of my seat, hitting my head on the overhead bin. Looking at my daughter and wife, they were both laughing at me. Pointing to my daughter and then pointing to the seat I just vacated, I gave her the switch sign. Passing my daughter in the aisle, she had a huge grin on her face. The last thing I heard from her was, *"Boy, are you lucky."*

Chapter 3

Camera Shop

July 1994, Rockford, Illinois

Outstanding! Hanging up the phone, I began telling my wife Christi that the 35mm lens I had dropped off for repair at the camera shop the week before was now ready for pickup. Excited to say the least, I snatched my wallet from the kitchen counter, grabbed the car keys, and headed out the front door. On my way through the kitchen, I noticed the wall clock was now showing 4:45 p.m. Through my mind, I quickly calculated the problem I was facing. I only had fifteen minutes to get to the camera shop before they closed at 5:00 p.m.

Hustling over to the car, I opened the driver-side door, jumped in, keyed the ignition, and started the car. Shifting into reverse, I knew that if all went well and if most of the stoplights were green, I could make the trip in a little over ten minutes. Stopping only occasionally, I was making good time. It seemed like the only thing against me was *time*! Pulling into the strip mall and parking just outside the camera shop, I noticed a man sitting on one of the available patrons' benches just inside the common mall area. Sitting in front of him was a slightly used chrome shopping cart, black plastic handle still intact with black rubber wheels. It was filled past the brim with bulging, assorted plastic bags and other assorted items that were indistinguishable from my vantage point. Not wanting to waste time because of the task at hand, I nervously found that my eyes were still drawn to him. Tan khaki pants and a dark-blue long-sleeved shirt with the sleeves rolled up to the elbow fit rather snugly to his bulky frame. Medium-length, shiny, coal-black hair was parted and sort of combed in multiple directions, giving him a minor unkept appearance. It looked obvious to me that this was a homeless man or at least had the appearance of one. Checking my watch, I had three minutes left till closing.

Wanting to help if I could, I briskly walked over to him and faced him as he sat on the bench. All I could say was, "Please stay here for a few minutes. I would like to talk to you, but I need to get to the camera shop before it closes." With that, I turned and started jogging over to the store. Within just a few seconds, I burst through the front door of the shop, acknowledging to myself the fact that the door wasn't locked.

Winding my way around display cases, I found my way to the back counter and handed the clerk my lens pickup ticket. While he searched for my lens, I thanked him for staying open a while longer to help me. He acknowledged my comment with a smile and a "You're welcome" then carefully handed me the camera lens. Removing the lens protector, I inspected its glass face and tried out its zoom capabilities. Everything was in order. Handing the lens back to the clerk, he neatly packaged it for me. I paid the bill while removing a twenty-dollar bill from my wallet, pocketed it, and began winding my way back to the front exit.

As I emerged from the camera shop, I was wondering if the homeless man was still perched on the pedestrian bench. Turning to my right, I spotted him still sitting where I had left him. Navigating the thirty feet or so to his resting spot, I sat down next to him. His face was rather plain and expressionless as I asked him what his name was.

He turned to face me and replied, "My name is Michael."

I exchanged my name with him and told him that I lived here in Rockford. I then asked him where he was from.

"Texas," was his reply.

Although that was not what I had expected, I accepted it at face value. I noticed that he spoke with a slight hesitation while having trouble forming his words. Not being very good at talking with a complete stranger, I reached into my pants pocket and removed the twenty-dollar bill. Asking him to accept it for food or whatever his needs were, he reached out with his right hand and took the twenty-dollar bill from me. He closed his hand while cradling the money and put his hand in his lap.

Not knowing what else to say, I got up and told him to take care of himself. As I rose up, he acknowledged my monetary gesture with a "Thank you." Walking back to the car, I was filled with unexplainable thoughts about what had just happened. I knew that it was the right thing to do. Besides, the last time something like this happened to me, I was walking through Chicago O'Hare Airport. Because of my initial rudeness to a gray-haired elderly woman, I had made a promise to God that I would never do that again. True to my word, I opened the car door, slid into the driver's seat, and with a smile etched on my face I turned to wave goodbye to the homeless man.

He was gone! The bench he was sitting on was empty. No him, no rubber-wheeled chrome cart, nothing. Shocked and flabbergasted, I knew that I had to find him. After all, I had twenty dollars invested in him. I exited the car and headed for the bench he was previously sitting on. While making this short walk, I scanned the sidewalk in front of the strip mall stores, hoping to see him. Nothing! I thought he might have gone into one of the mall stores, but my mind reasoned how he could have done that in a span of fifteen seconds. Running over to the left side of the mall closest to the bench, I rounded the corner, expecting to see him lazily pushing his cart down the sidewalk. Again, nothing!

I was deflated to say the least. I finally came to realize that he was gone, never to be seen again. I began to smile inside this time knowing that I had just helped an angel.

> Be not forgetful to entertain strangers: for thereby some have entertained angels unawares. (Heb. 13:2, KJV)

> Do not forget to show hospitality to strangers, for by so doing some people have shown hospitality to angels without knowing it. (Heb. 13:2, NIV)

Chapter 4

Jehovah's Witnesses (Zion, Illinois)

July 2001, Winthrop Harbor, Illinois

Serenity is a name that fits her well. She is the new top-of-the-line Sun Cruiser SCR 3300 from Maxum. It is a beauty of a boat. Thirty-six feet of fiberglass and chrome with a forward fitted radar arch, topped off with the latest in technology. Outfitted with the Raytheon Raymarine 4kw Radar Dome with combined GPS and scanner plotter allowed unlimited daylight or nighttime exploration. Fog, rain, wind, and waves were no match for the capabilities of this high-tech system. The MerCruiser Marine engines were configured with twin five-point-seven-liter 250 HP power plants. The combined 500 prop shaft HP with the super strong Bravo Two sterndrives allowed you to cruise at forty miles per hour on a calm lake. This boat was the perfect combination of size and muscle for the Great Lakes, especially for Lake Michigan.

Docked at Northpoint Marina in Winthrop Harbor, Illinois, it is the largest marina on the Great Lakes. It sports a protected floating dock system of 1,500 slips, dock lockers, electric power, potable water, and cable TV. What a way to spend a weekend.

Winthrop Harbor is a thriving village of 6,745 local residents nestled in the northeast corner of Lake County, Illinois. Bordering the Wisconsin State line, it is located forty-five miles north of Chicago. Winthrop Harbor is one of the finest tourist destinations in Illinois with its family-friendly beaches, parks, and shops.

It was an eighty-nine-degree day in late July, which was typical for that time of year. Being one o'clock in the afternoon, we knew that we were in for a scorcher. Having a late breakfast aboard the *Serenity* was a typical routine for a Saturday in the marina. We could hear bits and pieces of the other boaters' conversations through the three open portals located in the bow of the boat. Even in the early afternoon they spoke in hushed tones, not wanting to disturb anyone.

Finishing my last swallow of coffee, I told my wife Christi that I was going topside to open up the canvas enclosure surrounding the stern cockpit sitting area. Mounting the salon steps, I opened the door leading to the topside. Climbing the three steps, I was greeted by an infusion of white light from the noonday sun. Besides the bright sun, a crystalline wave of light was being reflected off of the sur-rounding water. In order to see, I had to squint my eyes into tiny slits to keep from going partially blinded by the sun. Finding my way to the stern access door, I opened it and stepped onto the three-foot swimming platform. Taking in a deep breath of lake air was like an elixir. I couldn't help but smile to myself on how fortunate we were to be here. Turning to the right, I walked over to the stern mooring line. Carefully stepping over it, I mounted the floating dock and turning toward the boat, began unsnapping the Sunbrella canvas and Isenglass windows. This routine, no matter how many times it was performed, never grew old. I thought, *This is the stuff boaters are made for.*

Finishing my task, I stowed the canvas in its respective lockers. Standing up, I was startled to see Christi standing behind me. Handing me my now-not-needed sunglasses, she quipped, "Here, you forgot these." Taking them from her, I put them on. I never said a word about her intended pun.

In the hot afternoon sun, we were now ready to go grocery shopping. Some tasks never change. Mounting the floating dock, we headed toward shore and the exit ramp leading to the security gate. Along the way, we had to dodge a couple of early-afternoon "dock dawgs." These were boaters who set out six to eight folding chairs adjacent to the middle of the eight-foot-wide dock, leaving a small pathway for you to walk down the middle. As we approached them, I noticed five pairs of sun-tanned legs protruding from various styles and colors of shorts with boaters' shoes adorning their feet. Boat shoes were also known as deck shoes. These shoes were typically constructed from canvas or leather and had nonmarking rubber soles. These shoes were stylish and "way cool" and were in vogue. Makers like Dockers Men's Castaway Boat Shoe or Tommy Hilfiger Bowman Boat Shoe can cost north of $100 a pair. Who cares what they cost if you're intent is to be "stylish?"

As we approached the dock dawgs, it was as if a make-shift bridge tender was in charge of legs. On cue from a hidden source of some kind, the five pairs of tanned legs began moving in unison away from the center of the dock. In a few seconds our pathway down the center of the dock was clear. Seeing this, Christi and I adjusted our two abreast walking style to two in line. Making sure Christi didn't inadvertently slap someone in the face with her purse, she removed it from the crook in her arm and held it in both hands out in front of her—not very comfortable but effective. With the obligatory "Excuse me," "Good afternoon," and "How are you?" out of the way, we successfully passed through this human gauntlet of boating fanatics.

Advancing down the dock, we passed through the metal gate on the ramp into the pedestrian walkway. With a clang, the gate closed behind us. Reaching our SUV, a gray GMC Jimmy, I keyed the fob in my hand, and with an audible click the doors unlocked. Opening the driver's-side door, I was greeted with a blazing blast of hot air. Cautioning Christi, I reached in with the keys, placed them in the ignition, and started the car. With a small roar the engine came to life. Reaching over to the center of the dash, I activated the AC's Maximum button and ducked back outside. Allowing a few minutes for the interior to cool down, we slid in unison onto the grey leather bucket seats. Clasping our seatbelts, I shifted into drive and carefully exited the parking lot.

The drive to the strip mall was about a ten-minute affair. Reaching the green traffic light on the four-lane main road through town, I cautiously turned left, accelerating to match the flow of cars heading into town. *Look for the McDonald's then four more blocks*, I thought to myself. The strip mall was on the left. Crossing the traffic and turning into the generous parking lot, I wound my way through a multitude of parked cars. Finding a vacant space at the head of the line, we parked, exited the car, and were greeted by another blast of heat. The solar heat off of the blacktop parking lot was intense. Thank goodness we had on our Walmart tennis shoes with the skid-resistant soles. Looking for cars, I glanced left and then right and began crossing the drive to Logan's Mini Mart.

As I glanced right, I noticed a man in front of a vacant store sitting on the walkway. Parked next to him was a rusty, red, twenty-six-inch bike with pitted chrome wheels and fenders that didn't match. His knees were tucked up to his chest, his arms around his legs, and his head tilted toward the ground. I couldn't tell if he was awake or sleeping. In this heat, just resting was a good idea. It had to be ninety degrees in the shade.

Entering the automatic doors of the store, we again found ourselves in cool air that had been dehumidified. It was almost cold inside. Overcoming a slight case of goosebumps, we entered the store and were greeted by multiple smells and aromas that can only be generated by a well-stocked grocery store. Coffee, milk, water, orange juice, cereal, fruit, and steaks for the grill were just some of the items we needed. Checkout went smoothly.

Bagged up and ready to go, we exited Logan's Mini Mart. Again, a rush of hot air hit us in the face, almost taking our breaths away. As we crossed the sticky blacktop, I again noticed to my left the man sitting on the walkway. He hadn't changed positions since I last saw him. Pointing him out to my wife, she, as I, was concerned for his welfare. Loading the groceries into the Jimmy and before closing the lift gate, I extracted two bottles of water from the case that we had purchased. I closed the lift gate and started walking in his direction. I had only taken a few steps when sweat began to drip off of my nose. *This man must be miserable*, I thought to no one in particular.

As I reached him, he sat up smiled, and said, "Hello." Seeing him smile, I thought was a good sign. He had cheery, intense blue eyes with bushy, gray eyebrows. A ball cap sat lazily on his head. Salt-and-pepper-grayish hair protruded from under the rim of the cap while slightly covering his ears. He was wearing a yellow, woolen tweed jacket with tan patches on the elbows. The coat was tattered and worn with the lower pockets bulging with who knows what. His light-gray collared dress shirt was a road map of wrinkles.

Standing there looking at him, I was amazed that there was no sweat on his face. Seeing this made no sense. A tweed jacket, ninety-degree heat, and no breeze—how could this be?

Feeling uncomfortable, I asked what his name was. He said it was Bill. I introduced myself and asked him if I could give him some water. He looked at the two plastic sixteen-ounce bottles of Ice Mountain Natural Spring Water I had cradled in my hands, and he simply said yes. For this I was grateful. Handing him the water, I mentioned to him to stay out of the sun and to stay hydrated. Thanking me for the water, I stood up, turned around, and started walking back to the car. By now my white short-sleeved polo shirt was slightly drenched from my profusely sweating back and chest. Back in the cool interior of the Jimmy, I updated my wife about the conversation I had with Bill. She asked me if Bill was homeless, which I did not know.

The rest of the weekend was more than pleasant for us. The slight lake breeze drifting through the boat and its perpetual eighty-degree temperature were just what the boaters asked for. We were already looking forward to the following weekend of boating.

Toughing out the work week was not new to us. The automotive components industry was filled with tragedy and triumphs. Parts for fuel injectors, parking brakes, and transmissions were just a few of the thousands of parts that were manufactured at our facility in Vernon Hills, Illinois. The high stress management of these types of operations was the main reason that weekend boating was so gratifying. Week in and week out it is the perfect way to reset your emotions in preparation for the following weeks of work.

Friday came, and we were ready for our castaway weekend with *Serenity* in Winthrop Harbor, Illinois. Since we never unpack the Jimmy, we only had to fight the rush-hour traffic, manage the unsettling pace of Interstate 94 traffic, pay our toll, and exit Highway 173 to Winthrop Harbor.

Having nothing to eat since lunch, we decided to stop at McDonald's in Winthrop Harbor. The "You Deserve a Break Today" was sounding pretty good. Pulling the Jimmy into the parking lot, I found a spot next to the side entrance. To our surprise, we saw Bill's rusty, red bike leaning against the building. Unlike our first meeting, there were overflowing multiple brown plastic bags hanging from its handlebars. They looked somewhat like stalactites in a cave hanging on for dear life. Unlike their mineral-deposit brothers, these bags were more than likely filled with personal belongings. It was now obvious that he was a homeless man. Getting out of the Jimmy, we had no more than closed the doors when he exited the side door that we were parked by. He walked toward his bike; that was where Christi and I intercepted him. Exchanging hellos, I introduced him to Christi. He warmly acknowledged her and said hello. Even in the dwindling light, his piercing blue eyes sparkled with enthusiasm. Bluer than a sapphire, they were clear and alert. After some small talk, we asked him where he was staying. He graciously acknowledged that an elderly lady named Dorothy was allowing him to stay on her enclosed back porch. He emphasized that it was a nice place for him to stay. He had no other explanation, nor was one needed.

As he said that, Christi's eyes got wide; and turning to me, she gave me a look of unbelief. It took me several seconds to realize what she wanted to say to me but not in Bill's presence. The reality that set in was that Bill and Dorothy were the names of her deceased parents. Christi was close beyond measure with her mother. They were closer friends than that of a sibling and parent. Even with five kids in her family, she had them all trumped when it came to Mom's attention.

It has been said that *coincidence is God's way of remaining anonymous.*

With a nod, I acknowledged my understanding of his statement to Christi. After a few minutes of engaging in additional small talk, Bill mounted his bike; and with a slight push with his right foot on the concrete walkway, he peddled away.

Our McDonald's dinner was uneventful and really quite peaceful. We didn't talk much. We were both lost in our own private thoughts of our evening experience with Bill. By the time we left the restaurant, the sun was setting in the western sky. An explosion of pinks, orangish reds, light blues, and grays covered the horizon as far as the north was from the south. The sun took center stage in the middle of this light show while preparing to give way to the night. Starting the Jimmy, we motored our way out of the parking lot onto the main road and headed for the harbor. Safely aboard *Serenity*, we decided to get up around 8:00 a.m. to get a head start on another upcoming beautiful day on Lake Michigan.

At breakfast, unbeknown to me, Christi was hatching out a plan to help Bill. Occasionally, her face contorted into a slight frown then a curious smile or on occasion simply a blank stare. Running out of Raisin Nut Bran cereal and rye toast, my curiosity finally got the best of me. "Honey, what are you thinking about," I finally asked her.

"Bill," was her reply." Continuing, she said, "I think we should buy him some toiletries. You know he was pretty grungy-looking."

I had to agree that this was a good idea. Rinsing our dishes in the sink, Christi grabbed her flip-flops and purse. I found my wallet, cell phone, and keys. Already wearing my Walmart tennis shoes with the skid-resistant soles, we were now ready to go. Mounting the dock, we immediately noticed that the dock dawgs were nowhere in sight. Left behind were a few beer bottles, some plastic cups, and couple of slightly ripped paper umbrellas that could be put into a mixed drink. The folding chairs were still intact with miscellaneous colored towels adorning the backs of the chairs. One of them, I'm sure, was a Betty Boop towel.

We made our way up the ramp, through the metal gate, and over to the parking lot. Finding the Jimmy, we started it up and left the parking lot behind us. Today, we were going to stop at the Jewel Food Store conveniently located on an access road behind the McDonald's to purchase the toiletries for Bill. The Jewel parking lot was at least half full. Parking near the middle center of the lot, I shut off the car and turned to Christi. I wanted to know what types of toiletries she had in mind. She answered with, "Just the basics." Accepting that, we exited the car, locked the doors, and started walking toward the entrance. Dodging a few cars on the way, we made it to the entrance and the automatic door. Stepping on the black matt, the door activated, jerking slightly as it opened with a rush of cool air. Grabbing a shopping cart, I maneuvered it past the displays, a flower kiosk, and the dog food aisle. As the cart rumbled down the main thoroughfare and noticing the "Paper Goods" sign, I hung a sharp left, almost running over a stock boy tending to organize one of the shelves displays. With a quick sorry, we moved on, only stopping when we reached the tissue products. Inquisitively, Christi started to scan the many brands to choose from. Not having shopped in years, I was amazed at the number of specific styles that were available—cleansing, absorbent, 2-ply, and ultrasoft, to name just a few. She opted for two boxes of the Kleenex Ultra-Soft. Wow! This was going to be a long day!

About twenty minutes later, we found ourselves in front of the toothpaste display. Christi turned toward me and in all seriousness asked me what kind I thought Bill would like. *You have to be kidding*, I thought to myself. I responded, "Get him the one with the green leaf on the box." Colgate Mint it was. Searching the personal products in a few more aisles, we were finally done. With our load now topped off, we headed for the checkout. Going into a checkout line was like a three-legged race. Coordination and timing were everything. At almost six feet two inches tall and 205 pounds, I was at an advantage. It wasn't all muscle, but there was just enough to manhandle the cart into any direction I wanted to go. The closer we got to the checkout, the faster I accelerated my pace. Passing slower shoppers, I found checkout number 2 to be my best choice. Glancing behind me, I noticed that Christi was lagging quite a way behind me. Giving her the "come on, catch up" arm wave, I turned back to the business at hand. Rounding the corner of the checkout, I parked parallel with the grocery conveyor on my first try. The woman in front of me had just finished paying for her purchases. Looking up at me, she gave me a relieved look. She was either glad that she had finished shopping or glad that I didn't run her over. My Walmart nonskid tennis shoes did their job perfectly.

Bellying up to the edge of the cart, I systematically began unloading it. I was about half done when Christi showed up. I gave her a quick smile and then allowed her to finish unloading the cart. I moved over to the cashier stand and watched as our purchases were scanned and rung up. After paying for them, I took the two plastic grocery bags from the packer, and we exited the store. Walking out the automatic doors, I noticed three bikes parked next to the exit. Sure enough, one of the bikes had rusty, red fenders with brown plastic bags hanging from the handlebars. I reasoned that when there was a bike, there had got to be a Bill not far behind.

We didn't have long to wait. A couple of minutes passed, and sure enough Bill exited the grocery store. He was still wearing the yellow woolen tweed jacket with tan patches on the elbows. The bulging pockets of his coat were now empty. He also wore a huge welcoming smile for me and Christi while holding a small bag with what appeared to be a sandwich in it. As we eyed the bag, he mentioned that on occasion the Jewel Store manager helped him out. Not wanting to embarrass him, we quickly changed the subject.

As it turned out, Bill was a master at the spoken word. He wasn't short on subjects either. We spent a good amount of time discussing the uncanny likelihood that his name was the same as Christi's father and that his friend Dorothy had the same name as her mother. What a coincidence that was. We bantered back and forth for a good thirty minutes when Christi finally said, "Bill, we have some gifts for you. We hope that you will accept them and use them as you see fit. If you don't want some of them, please give them to someone you know." With that, she handed Bill the two slightly overstuffed plastic bags of toiletries.

Looking inside each bag for a few seconds at a time, his eyes kept darting back and forth like a child eyeing his presents at Christmas. Reaching to the bottom of one bag, he clasped an item and gingerly brought out a small box of Q-tips. The smile on his face brightened into a large grin, and his sapphire-blue eyes shone brightly. Pantomiming the use of a Q-tip, he placed the whole box to his ear and pretended to clean his right ear that was partially hidden under his ball cap. Not working as well as he wanted with the Q-tip box, he shoved the side of his cap upward until it sat loosely on the crown of his head. With the cap now tilting at an awkward angle, he looked akin to an elderly Soupy Sales of the 1960s slapstick fame. With that, his smile only grew larger, now ear to ear. We laughed until our stomachs hurt. Tears were streaming down our faces.

After several minutes of worthy laughter, he readjusted his well-worn ball cap to its proper position, lowered his hand, and looked intently into my eyes. Feeling as if I had done something wrong, all I could do was stare at him. His eyes became intense. The smile and sparkle in his eyes were gone. He swallowed and lithely exhaled. With that he cleared his throat, opened his mouth, and began to speak.

"I need to tell you something about the Jehovah's Witnesses." Uttering those two words left me speechless. It turned out that for over a month, I had been intensely studying their beliefs and practices. Intrigued by what I had read, I kept looking for more articles to consume. Then I read,

> The Jehovah's Witnesses, regardless of their divergence from more mainstream doctrines, are a Christian faith. They

believe [italics added] in God, the creator, and that Jesus Christ is His son. However, they do not believe in the *Trinity* [italics added], the doctrine that God, Christ, and the Holy Spirit are all aspects of one God.[2]

This was unsettling, but I wanted to read more. The question was how did Bill know! I didn't have long to wait. He continued speaking. "I have been told to tell you that there is no need for you to study the Jehovah's Witnesses. God will deal with them in due time!" Shocked at the ramification of his words, I could only watch as he turned away, placed the two bags over the handlebars of his bike, and mounted the seat; and with a slight push with his left foot, he peddled away. Understanding what he said, I looked over at Christi. Her face was glowing with acknowledgement at what she had just heard. My mood brightened as I watched her wave to him as he rode away.

---

[2] Sunday Moultan, "Jehovah's Witnesses: Definition, Beliefs & Symbols," https://study.com/academy/lesson/jehovahs-witness-es-definition-beliefs-symbol.html.

Epilogue

Since meeting Bill, we returned to Winthrop Harbor almost every weekend but had yet to see him again. We had looked everywhere. I frequently reminded myself of those prophetic words that he startled me with that unforgettable day in July.

It was now September, and the days were getting shorter. The weather was getting a little brisk, and believe it or not the trees were turning from richly colored greens to a hazy sunset red. Sooner rather than later, we would have to put *Serenity* into dry dock for her winter solstice. Taken from us by the harshness of the Wisconsin winters, unlike Bill, we would see her soon.

SECTION 4

Demons in Scripture

Angels and Demons in Scripture

Satan hates God and God's people, and he is their enemy as well. While Satan has no power against God, he does have power against man and will do what he can to harm God's people. We must always be on guard for Satan or his demons' attacks. In most instances, these attacks will come during the day when we are awake and going about our days business. He continuously attempts to affect our thinking and ultimately our behavior. This will then become our standard of living that is contrary to the will of God. Never submit to circumstances but to the Lord who controls circumstances.

Let's look at several ways Satan can and will attack us:

1. He hinders us from our accepting Christ as Lord.

2. He hinders God's people from advancing the Lords agenda for the Body of Christ.

3. Sexual temptation for those who are having difficulties with self-control.

4. He will cause division among believers. These divisions are usually based upon a wrong understanding of Scripture.

5. Satan is the father of false teachings. Have you ever asked yourself why there are so many different denominations of churches?

6. Satan will choose victims who are alone or are not alert to his devious ways.

7. Attacks will come during suffering or persecutions that we may be going through. Many times, Satan will tempt us to blame God for our suffering.

8. When believers feel alone, weak, helpless, and cut off from other believers, they can become so focused on their troubles that they forget to watch out for danger.

9. Fear, depression, and worry on our part will attract Satan to attack us.

Neither give place to the devil. (Eph. 4:27)

> Submit yourselves therefore to God. Resist the devil, and he will flee from you. (James 4:7)

The Old Testament gives us an understanding of what Satan does on a daily basis. The New Testament tells us to be sober and vigilant because of Satan's unrelenting tactics.

> And the Lord said unto Satan, Whence comest thou? Then Satan answered the Lord, and said, From going to and fro in the earth, and from walking up and down in it. (Job 1:7)

> Be sober, be vigilant; because your adversary the devil, as a roaring lion, walketh about, seeking whom he may devour. (1 Pet. 5:8)

Jesus died on the cross to defeat Satan, who had the power of death. Christ had to die because only by dying could he break the power of the devil.

> Forasmuch then as the children [us] are partakers of flesh and blood, he [Jesus]

also himself likewise took part of the same;
that through death he might destroy him
[Satan] that had the power of death, that
is, the devil. (Heb. 2:14)

Therefore, Peter and Paul urged the believers to always be alert for Satan's tricks. Be prepared and put on the whole armor of God (see Section 7).

Demons That Attack during Sleep

In your dreams, have you ever been unable to move or you have that awful feeling of being crushed or something heavy was on your chest, making it impossible for you to breathe? Most likely, you partially woke up and cried out to Jesus for help, and you could then breathe again. Have you ever had a demonic attack in a dream and then woke up, wondering why it happened? Satan does not explain his reasons for the attack. These dreams must be interpreted based on their content. During these dreams, you more than likely felt scared and alone and unable to get help. Being anxious would be an understatement.

Demonic attacks can fit into two categories. As previously stated, let's look again at the first category or ways that Satan can and will attack us.

Category 1—Personal, physical, spiritual, mental

1. He hinders us from our accepting Christ as Lord.

2. He hinders God's people from advancing the Lord's agenda for the Body of Christ.

3. Sexual temptation for those who are having difficulties with self-control.

4. He will cause division among believers. These divisions are usually based upon a wrong understanding of Scripture.

5. Satan is the father of false teachings. Have you ever asked yourself why there are so many different denominations of churches?

6. Satan will choose victims who are alone or are not alert to his devious ways.

7. Attacks will come during suffering or persecutions that we may be going through. Many times, Satan will tempt us to blame God for our suffering.

8. When believers feel alone, weak, helpless, and cut off from other believers, they can become so focused on their troubles that they forget to watch out for danger.

9. Fear, depression, and worry on our part will attract Satan to attack us.

Category 2

This category is just the opposite of the category 1 descriptions. We are at peace with God, Jesus, and the Holy Spirit. As an example, if we encounter false teachings, we are eager to search the scriptures for the true meaning. We promote unity among believers, not division.

1. Scripturally strong
2. Spiritually healthy
3. Strong faith
4. Biblical teaching—Jesus's shed blood
5. Embrace new Scripture revelations
6. Believe in eternal life

Why would someone in category 2 suffer demonic attacks? It is because of the strong belief system given to us by God. However, these attacks are physical in nature and are intended to hurt or inflict painful and severe injuries on the body by maiming or killing the believer. Yes, Satan has this ability to do this. I speak for myself personally.

I have been attacked in my dreams physically for three times and emotionally for two times. In each case, the satanic attempt was to keep me from teaching Christ. Each attempt was a coordinated effort to get me to stop teaching and give up Jesus.

Scripture is basically silent on the element of demonic attacks and how to deal with them when they take place in your dreams. Yes, Satan can and does take over your dreams. He can also physically attack your body when you are asleep. Let me share with the reader these abilities and four real-life stories that are associated with them.

1. He can blend into an existing dream to make you unaware of the coming attack.

2. In my case, Satan attacked only at night.

3. His spiritual form can remain unseen while doing you physical harm or destruction to your surroundings.

4. He can enter our realm of space and time from the one he is now in.

5. In my instance, there was no verbal communication given.

6. The faces of my demonic attackers, although very ugly, were expressionless.

SECTION 5

Demon Encounters

Chapter 1

Case of Strangulation (Nightstand Blues)

The next thing I heard was, "Time to eat." My wife woke me out of a fully focused discussion I was having with myself on salvation and how to conclude Saturday Bible studies. I decided on using the tried-and-true summary of the key elements of the discussion. I would top this off with the companion verses on salvation found in Romans 10:8–11.

Dinner was a little different that Thursday night. I took the opportunity to share these Gospel passages with my wife and their implication on our lives. With a pert smile only she could give and a slight nod of her head, she signified agreement.

God had been opening my eyes to these passages and other supporting scripture for about five months. It's not

117

that I was a slow learner. It's just that like others, I was hung up on the four Gospels. Venturing out of them and into the scriptural arena with the apostle Paul was a little terrifying. For about the first week, I had a severe case of paradigm paralysis. It was difficult accepting anything new. But God did not give up. It was apparent that he was not finished with me yet. The days of keeping the Law and ordinances are over. We only need to ask the Lord, and he will give you understanding in all things.

After dinner, my wife and I watched a little news and weather. At 10:20 p.m. she almost made it to the weather, but I looked over and found her fast asleep. Waking her, I then went and got ready for bed. Being Thursday, I was mentally bushed—enough excitement for one day.

Brushing teeth, washing hands and face, and combing hair were a routine established by my mother over many years. I could never figure out the comb-your-hair routine. I used to tell her that it was only going to get messed up by my pillow. Unlike my mother, I was used to a good case of "bed head." Over the years I decided that the word *infinity* described this moment. No two bed heads were alike. I finally crawled into bed at 11:00 p.m. and talked to God for about fifteen minutes before falling asleep.

The dream I remember from that night was confusing to say the least. About fifteen to twenty people, male and female, dressed in a rainbow of muted colors were walking from the left side of my vision to the right on a black floor. Where they were going, I did not know. It was a dream without a destination, just a wall of grayish black in front of them. I was walking about fifteen feet behind this group but could clearly see them all. Their backs were to me, and I was walking toward them but at a slight angle so I could catch up. What seemed like a few minutes was about to be turned into a long-term nightmare.

Suddenly and without warning, the grayish-black background turned light gray and red-speckled. It reminded me of a cheap wallpaper, and with that I stopped walking toward the crowd. With the same suddenness, a figure off to the left of my vision at about thirty feet away came to my attention. This was not a person that had been in the crowd of people.

It was a thing of unimaginable weirdness. It looked like it was about five feet tall with no clothes or facial features. It had a rounded, elongated body and two arms and two legs, with hands that looked like they wore two fingered mittens with a thumb. It was totally violet in color and smooth like glass. Its eyes were not that of a human and were featureless; they were light purple in color with dark-purple eyebrows. There was no sign of hair on its oval head, but it too was violet in color. By now, this thing was walking straight for me. Its legs were slowly pumping out a walking rhythm, but they did not bend because there were no knees. The violet mukluk-covered feet never touched the black floor but maintained the semblance of walking while getting closer and closer. I thought that this was all horribly wrong, and while never taking my eyes off of it, I felt myself turning to my left so it was approaching my right side and arm. Before my next thought matured in my mind, it was upon me. A heavy two-fingered hand grasped the top of my left shoulder. Its right hand grabbed my upper-right arm and forced me to turn, so my back was now facing it.

In one fluid motion, it wrapped its right arm around my neck so that the bicep of its right arm covered the front portion of my throat under my chin. Its wrist and two-fingered right hand lay against my left ear and jaw-bone. Clasping both hands, palms together, and interlocking its thumbs, I found I was now in a classic choke hold. The strength of this abomination was staggering. Breathe!

I can't breathe! I grabbed and tugged at its muscular right arm with both of my hands to no avail. I was in dire straits, and I knew I only had seconds to live.

In an instant, I reached up with my right arm, contorted my elbow and wrist, and wrapped my arm around the back of its head. In one motion I leaned forward, dropping all my weight to my knees, forcing this thing's weight onto my back. Pulling down as hard as I could, I found that leverage was on my side; and flipping it over my right shoulder, its grip started to loosen. As we slowly rotated over, I felt gravity take hold as I was falling forward down into a bottomless black pit. Seconds seemed to pass. Then with a thud, I hit the bottom of the pit, landing flush on the crown of my head. The pain I felt was intense, but it wasn't done yet. The momentum I had generated caused my chest, buttocks, and legs to unravel in front of me. My eyes popped open, but I could only see black. My head throbbed with every beat of my heart. I was lying on my back on the carpeted floor of the bedroom.

Without warning, a bright flash of light dilated my eyes to the extent that I still could not see. Squinting through two small slits, I peered over to my right side, looking for "it." As far as I knew, this fight was still not over yet. It was gone! The light that had blinded me was emanating from a lamp situated on the end table next to the bed. My wife was kneeling at my left side, asking if I was okay.

I assured her that I was okay, except for the throbbing in my head. After taking stock of each body part, I sat up and leaned against the bed frame. I ached all over. I felt like I had just gone over Niagara Falls in a barrel. Having an elevated bed, it was over three feet from the top of the mattress to the floor. My wife asked what had happened with me ending up falling off the bed on my head. I described to her the events leading up to this moment. She was shocked to fully understand the meaning of what had happened and tried assuring me that it was only a dream.

I knew that this was not the case. Yes, this was a dream in the beginning, but it had rapidly deteriorated into a physical demonic attack. The weight on my back was real. The arm around my throat and the fact that I could not breathe were real. Looking at the nightstand, I noticed that the time on the digital clock was 4:10 a.m., Friday morning. Looking further down, I saw that the right-hand side of the double doors on the nightstand was obliterated. It was in three vertical pieces lying on the inside of the cabinet with its hinges torn from the frame. There was only one way this could have happened: the "it" in my dream must have done this in frustration for not accomplishing its goal of killing or maiming me.

Epilogue

After a few more minutes of contemplating what had taken place, I final got off of the floor, stood up on my tip-toes, and sat on the edge of the bed. I knew that this attack was real and not just a dream. We had physical evidence to prove it. Yet I found myself unnerved by this incident. I was attacked in a dream! Satan had taken over my dream and tried orchestrating its outcome to fit his sick desires and goal. I was able to put the facts together and found that by teaching the shed blood of Jesus was more than Satan could take. In my strength, Satan was trying to find weakness. What he found was spiritual determination supported by God and Christ.

I didn't sleep anymore that night. There was no doubt that God was with me. He gave me the strength and endurance to fight off this demonic intruder and the attempt on my life. I knew that my life from this moment on would be changed forever. Although a little afraid, I prayed to God for strength to endure.

Chapter 2

High-Powered Rifle

Those who study sleep and sleep cycles say that the standard figure given for the average length of the sleep cycle in an adult man is 90 to 120 minutes.

N1 (nonrapid eye movement [stage 1]) is when the person is drowsy or awake to falling asleep. Brain waves and muscle activity start to decrease at this stage.

N2 is when the person experiences a light sleep. Eye movement has stopped by this time. Brain-wave frequency and muscle tonus are decreased. The heart rate and body temperature go down.

N3 or even N4 are the most difficult stages to be awakened. Every part of the body is now relaxed; breathing, blood pressure, and body temperature are reduced.

The National Sleep Foundation discusses the different stages of NREM sleep and their importance. *They describe REM* [rapid eye movement] *sleep as "a unique state in which dreams usually occur. The* brain is awake and body paralyzed." This unique stage is usually when the person is in the deepest stage of sleep and dreams. (Wikipedia; italics added)

h t t p s : / / e n . w i k i p e d i a . o r g > w i k i > R a p i d _ e y e _ movement_sleep

If deep sleep is about the body, *REM* is about the brain.

That night, I must have been very active in REM sleep if this is where dreams occur. We do not know when Satan can attack you in your dreams. Since these attacks are varied in time and space, you can't track them.

It had been four nights since my encounter with the first demon. Since I don't remember them, my dreams from those nights are inconsequential—just the way I like them. I must admit that I was a little nervous going to sleep each night since then.

Around 11:00 p.m. to 11:30 p.m., I finally decided that it was time to go to bed. My eleven-hour day had been long and hardworking on several quotes for my part-time business of building decks, pergolas, and arbors. After quoting, I usually had to visit the job site we were working on.

Following the approved set of engineering drawings, my three contract workers were self-starters and did fabulous work with little or no supervision. You would think that after days like this, going to sleep would not be a problem.

After fluffing my pillows, I finally tucked myself in. Laying my head down, I felt contented and ready for sleep. *No problems tonight*, I thought. With that, I closed my eyes and was instantly asleep. I usually spend ten to fifteen minutes talking to God before falling asleep. Tonight would be different.

The demonic dream tonight followed the same pattern as the previous attacks. Suddenly and without warning, the grayish-black background turned light gray and red speckled. Again, it reminded me of a cheap wallpaper. There was no floor or one that could be discerned. It was filled with black space, a bottomless pit to nowhere. Except for the wall background, I felt as if I was floating in place. Nothing was visible—no people, buildings, or objects of any kind. Yet before my eyes a shape of some sort began taking form. Fluorescent silver and green lines began to appear, taking on various shapes of some sort of object; the first one was a line then another and another. Before long, I could make out what looked like the outline of a long-sleeved shirt.

Its cuffs rolled up to where an elbow might be. The shirt was colored dark gray and outlined only by these fluorescence green lines without spot or wrinkle. With every line that was added, the intensity of the light became that of a shooting star in a clear night sky. My curiosity was peaked but with an added sense of foreboding.

Instantly, the lines stopped forming, with an explosion of intense green and white lights. It appeared so fast that it permeated my visual spectrum of sight. It ended as fast as it started. I was now looking at a side view of a hideous-looking person holding a high-powered rifle in a firing position. Mounted above the rifle's bolt-action mechanism was a telescopic site with what looked like three-inch lenses. The figure was lying in a prone position, resting on its elbows, with its contorted face turned toward me. Its ugliness was so frightening that I had a difficult time looking at it. Its green-outlined eyes bore through me like a hot knife through butter.

Its fluorescent-green-outlined hair was matted in round clumps like four-inch dreadlocks sticking up and outward on the crown of its head and sides while covering its ears. This porcupine look matched the overgrown, shaggy, spiked eyebrows. Its mouth and lips were closed but with a smirk emanating through what I was sure were clenched gritted teeth. The muscles in its cheeks flexed with a future anticipation. Its hands were as gross as its face. They were not proportioned at all. The bony knuckles were much larger than the meatless finger bones. Its right-hand thumb was wrapped around the neck of the gunstock; its scrawny fingers gripped underneath. Its right index finger inserted through the trigger guard rested on the trigger in a firing position. The left hand was under the front portion of the stock in a cradling position under the barrel. The rifle clarity was crisp and intentional so as to intimidate. Every detail was illuminated, enhancing this intimidation factor.

As if by command, this living silhouette and its rifle began turning ninety degrees to the right toward me! Its body did not move, but the turning continued. It appeared to be on an unseen ghostly turntable of some sort. As it rotated toward me, its face and head maintained its gruesome look while maintaining its probing eye contact with me. If it was looking for a weakness, it didn't have to. I was scared to death.

My heart started to pound, and my breathing quickened, as I now realized it was going to kill me. I was the intended target. I was now about three feet from the end of the barrel's muzzle. Trying to move forward to grab the rifle barrel, I found my leg muscles paralyzed. In a burst of sheer terror, I commanded them to move, but it was useless. The apparition continued to rotate toward me. I felt its presence getting closer and closer like the sickening stench of rotting meat. But it seemed like there was nothing I could do. A few more degrees of rotation and the muzzle would be pointing at my head! In an act of desperation, I began waving my outstretched arms in front of me, my fingers fully extended, trying to knock the rifle aside. Back and forth…back and forth…but my arms were too short by inches. The rotation stopped. The barrel of the rifle was now aimed at my head. Back and forth…back and forth—

"Honey! Honey, wake up!"

My eyes opened to a dim light coming from above me. I was sprawled on the bed facedown on top of the covers with my arms hanging over the side. The apparition was gone. Breathing with short, quick gasps of air, I found myself on the verge of hyperventilating. "Breathe in, breathe out," I said to myself. Slowly my senses were returning to normal. Until that moment, I didn't realize how good it felt to be alive. Sitting up, I looked over at the digital clock on the nightstand. It read 4:25 a.m.

Chapter 3

Most Favorite Dog, Sammy 2

It is a fact that Satan can attack you physically, emotionally, mentally, or spiritually. If you are attacked physically, the other three are automatically involved. An example would be when if you suffer a physical demonic attack, you may ask yourself, "Why did God allow this to happen to me?" If for example you are attacked spiritually, you may get emotionally or mentally distraught or suffer from a physical aliment.

I have had three dogs named Sammy in my life. Sammy 1 and 2 were purebred keeshonden. They were rescue dogs. In Hebrew, Sam or Sammy means "God has heard." I always felt that was rather special and unique.

> The Keeshond is a handsome, fluffy-looking dog with an intelligent expression and a foxlike face. It has a lion-like ruff and thickly coated rear end, forming characteristic "trousers." (Petmd.com)

> Keeshonds have a sweet temperament, making them good companion dogs. If

you live in a small apartment, a keeshond is a great choice because he doesn't require a lot of space to be happy... As a breed, keeshonds grasp obedience well, and behave well when properly trained. [3]

They cuddle.

In addition to providing companionship to workers on barges, the breed also has a long history of taking care of children and acting as babysitters. As adults, Kees weigh in at around 40 to 50 lbs, but that does not stop them from wanting to be lap dogs.[4]

[3] Caryn Anderson, "Are Keeshonds Good Dogs?" https://dogcare. dailypuppy.com/keeshonds-good-dogs-6606.html.

[4] Chelsea Tomat, "Life with a Keeshond," last modified December 26, 2013, https://www.petnaturals.com/blog/life-with-a-keeshond/.

Unfortunately, Sammy 1 and 2 have passed. Then after some time my wife and I had to have a Sammy 3. This time, it was a rescued purebred tan-and-black German shepherd or GSD.

> The German shepherd dog is a herding breed known for its courage, loyalty and guarding instincts. This breed makes an excellent guard dog, police dog, military dog, guide dog for the blind and search and rescue dog. For many families, the German shepherd is also a treasured family pet.[5]

> German shepherd dogs (GSD) are noble, diligent, loyal, and highly intelligent dogs. They are large in size [Sammy 3 weighs in at 103 pounds] and have very streamlined, athletic builds that make them both strong and agile. They also make highly effective guard dogs. Of course, the German shep-

---

[5] "German Shepherd Dog Breed Information and Personality Traits," https://www.hillspet.com/dog-care/dog-breeds/german-shepherd.

herd dog also makes a wonderful companion in the right home.[6]

This story and its subsequent demonic attack will
show you the lengths that Satan will go to. Nothing is out
of bounds for him and his demons. He will do everything;
he can to make you suffer emotionally, physically, or spiritually. In this instance, he targeted Sammy 2, even though
he had passed several years before.

Sammy 2 was very obedient and a happy-go-lucky
keeshond. At fifty-five pounds, he was a little on the heavy
side. All muscle, I used to say. We were the best of friends.
We used to romp and play in the house all the time. He
would run around a wall separating the kitchen and dining
room from the family room. He really thought he was hot
stuff.

One day, I was shelling and eating salted peanuts while
watching a football game on TV. I was cracking the shells
with my teeth to get at the nuts inside. Well, curiosity got

---

[6] Jenna Stregowski, RVT, "German Shepherd: Dog Breed
Profile," updated October 8, 2019, https://www.thes-
prucepets.com/breed-profile-german-shepherd-dog-
1117967.

the best of him, and Sammy came over and sat at my feet watching me shell peanuts. I gave him a couple of the nuts, and he loved them. Sitting on the floor next to him, I had decided to teach him how to shell peanuts. Trust me when I say I had his full attention, especially when a treat was involved.

Taking one out of the bag, I showed it to him and let him smell the shell. That being accomplished, I placed the peanut between my teeth and showed it to him. I found that, that was a mistake because he thought that it was his, and he grabbed it out of my mouth; and in doing so he slobbered all over my face. I told him no, and he dropped the saliva-covered peanut onto the carpet.

Taking another peanut out of the bag, I began the same routine. Once the peanut was between my teeth, I raised my hand, palm facing him, which meant "wait." Watching intently, I then proceeded to bite down on the peanut. Hearing the audible crack of the shell, Sammy decided to bark at me. This was a keeshond's way of saying, "Yeah, yeah, I got it already." Wanting to take advantage of this opportunity, I removed the peanut from my mouth, finished cracking it open, and laid the two peanuts on the carpet at his feet. I made sure he observed everything I was doing.

I then placed the two half shells next to the two peanuts. Pointing at the two peanuts, I then commanded him by saying, "Okay," which meant to him that he could now eat them. He immediately grabbed the two peanuts and chewed once, maybe twice, and then down the hatch they went. Tentatively, he then eyed the two remaining shells, looking at me and then at the shells. Picking up the two shells, I patted him on the head and told him, "Good Sammy." His response was another bark, which in Sammy language meant, "Give me another peanut." Obliging him, I took another jumbo peanut from the bag, let him smell it, and then gave it to him.

He took the peanut from me and promptly lay down next to me. With that, I heard a crunch then several more. I thought for sure that he was eating the peanut. To my surprise, he spit the peanut out. He looked at the four to five pieces on the carpet, and with his paw and mouth he started separating the shell from the peanuts! Success! I had all I could do to believe with my eyes. Sammy was one smart dog. By now you may be wondering what a dog named Sammy has to do with a demonic attack. The point is that it has everything to do with it.

I don't remember any of the dreams I had that night, except one. In my mind's eye, I was in a room with blackish-gray walls, ceiling, and floor. I felt as if I was floating in this space. Without warning, the far wall turned from blackish gray to light gray and red-speckled. I felt an almost-suffocating anxiety come over me. This was the same pattern of events I had previously experienced, yet I couldn't wake up. To me, this was real. Small, fluffy, pillowed clouds colored white and blue began to appear on the red-speckled wall one after another, almost in slow motion yet in unison. They seemed to layer themselves together in the shape of an irregular square with white light emanating from around and behind the clouds.

From within the center of the clouds, there was an eruption of color and a form taking shape. Several seconds passed. Then before my eyes, Sammy appeared. He was hanging limply from a taut rope around his neck. The rope was attached to nothing and was just hanging there in midair. I cried out to him, but there was no movement. *Run! Run!* I thought. My legs seemed paralyzed, unable to move. They would not respond to this horrific scene in front of me. I knew I had only seconds to act. I reached out to him in desperation. I called out, "Sammy…"

Instantly, the gruesome picture vanished. My eyes were open; my arms were outstretched before me. I was sitting up in bed while darkness surrounded me. I was breathing heavily. I desperately wanted to check on Sammy to make sure he was okay. In that microsecond, I was crushed to realize that I couldn't help him. He didn't exist except in my memory. He had passed several years earlier.

It's been about two years since this demonic attack, yet the picture of Sammy hanging in midair is still with me today. Yes, it may occupy a place in my memory as terrible as it was, but Satan lost. Every time I think about eating peanuts, a smile comes to my face, for those days will never be forgotten.

Chapter 5

Kick in the Lower Back

It was in late March of 2017 when my daughter, Alissen; her son, Owen, who was six; and her daughter, Ava, who was eight; and I accepted an invitation from my son, Matthew, to visit him. The only caveat was that we lived in Round Lake, Illinois, and he was having a house built in Murfreesboro, Tennessee. Driving for eight hours was not my idea of a good time. Not only could we check out his new house, but we could also stop at Metropolis, Illinois, and visit Superman.

Working at the General Motors plant in Spring Hill, Tennessee, this was a short twenty-five-minute commute for him. His wife and three children were still living in Roscoe, Illinois, waiting for the house to be finished and the school year to end. We could definitely help with the separation anxiety that we were sure he was feeling.

Our drive to Tennessee was a little boring with a little construction and some heavy traffic, which meant that the whole thing was uneventful. We opted to stop and visit Superman on the return trip home.

We arrived in Murfreesboro at approximately 4:30 p.m. on Thursday. Matt had taken up residence at the Days Inn where he had been staying for the last month or so. I would be staying with Matt on the sleeper sofa. Needing a pool for the children, Alissen checked in at the Fairfield Inn that was across the street.

It was good to see Matt. It had been a few months since we last saw him. On this occasion, he looked a little different. He had gained weight—not the plump kind but the muscle kind. As a young child, he had always been all arms and legs with very little in the middle. At six feet one inch, he was a tad on the skeletal side with eyes. Now he looked a little north of 180 pounds. Since there was nothing else to do, Matt told us that he was working out at a local gym every night, and it showed.

By now, it was 6:00 p.m. and time for supper. Needing a superfood, we opted for the Texas Roadhouse steak house where we were sure to be reenergized by one of their hand-cut steaks, drinks, and of course, line dancing.

> Country dancing is an integral part of the
> Texas Roadhouse experience.

"We line dance every hour on the half hour," restaurant owner Mike Parratino said. "It's just something fun for the guests. It's just part of what we do at Texas Roadhouse, have some fun and keep the energy up and guests love it."[7]

True to their word, the line dancing was lively, the food was great, and the service was awesome.

Driving back to the hotel was a little on the quiet side for us all. Being tired from our eight-hour, 556-mile drive that day had us in a sleepy and somewhat somber mood. We were all looking forward to a good night's rest. Arriving at the hotel, Matt and I grabbed my suitcase and other belongings and headed for his room. It turned out that they had put him up in a suite on the sixth floor but only charged him the standard room rate. It had everything to do with his frequent stayer status. Like flying, it had its perks.

---

[7] Dion Feller, "The dance was illegal at Wichita's new Texas Roadhouse, but now it's not," last updated March 8, 2018, https://www.kansas.com/news/politics-government/article204213149.html.

His room was not spectacular, but it had all the amenities required for a long-term stay—refrigerator, microwave, cupboards, and stove, along with a separate sitting area for reading or watching TV. It also had Wi-Fi, a desk, and a well-padded office chair. The walls were tan in color and slightly muted to keep from overpowering the size of the room. Artwork was sparse but did compliment the room's furniture.

Getting ready for bed was the same routine as always—bathroom, brushing of teeth, combing of hair, and washing of face. Mom would be so proud of me. The sleeper sofa turned out to be queen-size, a lot bigger than I needed. I learned in the army that if I curled up just right, I could sleep on a postage stamp. Making the bed was arduous. The sheets must have been for a king-size bed. Tucking in all of the extra sheet left small lumps in the bed under the mattress. Finding this unacceptable, I decided to smooth out an area large enough for me to sleep in and call it a night. Crawling into bed, I found it reasonably comfortable.

Since I had previously endured three demonic attacks while sleeping, tonight I decided to pray extra special. The last few months had been difficult to deal with. Ever since I started teaching the Bible study group about all things pertaining to Jesus, Satan had, had me in a special set of demonic sights. I was convinced that he would do anything to silence me.

I specifically remember praying to God for protection while I was dreaming so Satan could not be allowed to affect my dreams at any time that night. This prayer and its associated specifics lasted for at least fifteen minutes. In the ending, I prayed through the authority and in the name of Jesus Christ, my Lord! I felt that I was now ready for sleep. Little did I know that this night would be filled with physical and emotional suffering.

It was about 10:30 p.m. when I drifted off to sleep. I am sure that I was in full NREM (nonrapid eye movement) sleep within twenty minutes. The experts tell us that N3 or even N4 are the most difficult stages to be awakened.

The attack came without any warning! I was facing the interior of the bed as I slept on my left side. There was a crushing blow to my back from the top of my shoulders to the small of my back. It was a solid object of massive intensity. During impact, it slid my whole body approximately six-inches from its original sleeping position. The enormous pain was emanating from my back through my rib cage to the full front of my body. During impact, I remember trying to wake up. I felt like I was in a long tunnel with only blackness as my guide. The muscles in my back were racked with pain, yet the pain was forcing me into consciousness. Reasoning was starting to reassert itself into my semiconscious state. At that moment, I realized I was not at home or in my own bed. Neither was I dreaming. The pain was physical, not mental. In an instant, my heart started racing, blood pressure skyrocketing. The pit of my stomach ached with the rush of adrenaline when I realized it was *Satan*!

I feared for my life, yet I refused to move, open my eyes, or turn over to see who or what had caused this to happen. I was determined not to give the adversary any reason to strike again. This much I knew. Satan was in our physical world. He was not part of any dream or nightmare. This was real, not mystical or ghostly in nature. After three to four minutes, I was fully awake, but I kept my eyes closed. My breathing and heart rate returned to near normal. The searing pain in my back was subsiding. Scared but determined, I nonchalantly turned over to my right side. Holding still for a few seconds, I finally opened my eyes and was greeted with the dull luminescence of a dark room. Quickly focusing my eyes, I saw nothing out of the ordinary. The attack had run its course.

Realizing that I was safe, even with a painful back, I was mad—not sinning mad, just mad. I had prayed for this not to happen. Or did I?

Epilogue

I needed to answer that question, "Or did I?" I had prayed that Satan would not be allowed to affect my dreams and that he should not be allowed to harass me emotionally or hurt me physically. On those two accounts, God did protect me. I never dreamed that Satan could enter our physical world and cause grief, pain, or even death. This just made no sense. Are we to pray to God and have grievous things still happen to us? I know that this is unlikely because God will not tempt us. Jesus suffered and was tempted by Satan. Because of this, Jesus can help us during these times.

> When tempted, no one should say, "God is tempting me." For God cannot be tempted by evil, nor does he tempt anyone. (James 1:13)

No temptation has overtaken you except
what is common to mankind. And God
is faithful; he will not let you be tempted
beyond what you can bear. But when you
are tempted, he will also provide a way out
so that you can endure it. (1 Cor. 10:13)

Because he [Jesus] himself suffered when
he was tempted, he is able to help those
who are being tempted. (He. 2:18)

It was several days before the answer came to me. God
has given us a reality check in the story of Job. That is
why the two stories are included in this book. To me, it is
now perfectly simple. In the story of Job, Satan complained
to God that he had set a "hedge" of holy angels around
Job, his family, and his possessions. Satan and his demons
could not penetrate this spiritual hedge. Now, when I pray,
I include asking God to provide a hedge of his holy angels
around me, my family, and my possessions. I go so far as to
name everyone in our family whom I am praying for.

It has been two and a half years since this last and most
devastating demonic attack. Two weeks after the attack, my
doctor prescribed a muscle relaxant and physical therapy. I

am also restricted to twenty-five pounds of carrying weight. My back still hurts at times, but no medications are necessary. I stay busy by studying the Word of God, working as his ambassador for the Body of Christ and teaching his Word during Bible studies.

SECTION 6

Satan's Scriptural Nightmares

Biblical Truths That Caused the Attacks

Topic 1

Gospel of Salvation

The gospel of salvation has its roots in the current age of grace we now live in. I have talked to hundreds of people who do not know that the way of salvation is through the shed blood of Christ, his resurrection, and his ascension to heaven. The gospel is instead found in 1 Corinthians 15:1–4 and not in Matthew, Mark, Luke, or John through a mystery (secret) that only Paul new. Yes, God has kept secrets from men until the time for them to be fulfilled has come.

> The secret *things belong* unto the Lord our
> God: but those *things which are* revealed

belong unto us and to our children forever… (Deut. 29:29; italics added)

Moreover, brethren, I [Paul], declare unto
you the gospel which I preached unto you,
which also ye have received, and wherein
ye stand.

By which also ye are saved, if ye keep
in memory what I preached unto you,
unless ye have believed in vain.

For I delivered unto you first of all
that which I also received, how that Christ
died for our sins according to the scriptures

And that he was buried, and that he
rose again the third day according to the
scriptures. (1 Cor. 15:1–4)

Salvation companion verse

"That if thou shalt confess with thy mouth the Lord
Jesus, and shalt believe in thine heart that God hath raised
him from the dead, thou shalt be saved.

For with the heart man believeth unto righteousness; and with the mouth confession is made unto salvation" (Rom. 10:9–10).

Topic 2

Christian Origination

"And when he had found him [Paul], he brought him unto Antioch. And it came to pass, that a whole year they assembled themselves with the church [Body of Christ], and taught much people. And the disciples were called [by the Gentiles] Christians first in Antioch" (Acts 11:26).

Topic 3

Apostle Peter and the Christians

Paul was the apostle to the Gentiles, and Peter was the apostle to the Jews. Peter was not the first pope. If he was, he would be a Jewish pope, under the law.

> And I [Paul] went up by revelation, and communicated unto them that gospel which I preach among the Gentiles, but privately to them which were of reputa-

tion, lest by any means I should run, or had run, in vain.

But contrariwise, when they saw that the gospel of the uncircumcision [Gentiles] was committed unto me [Paul], as *the gospel* of the circumcision [Jew] *was* unto Peter;

(For he that wrought effectually in Peter to the apostleship of the circumcision, the same was mighty in me [Paul] toward the Gentiles:)

And when James, Cephas, and John, who seemed to be pillars, perceived the grace that was given unto me [Paul], they gave to me and Barnabas the right hands of fellowship; that we *should go* unto the heathen, and they unto the circumcision. (Gal. 2:2, 7–9; italics added)

For I speak to you Gentiles, inasmuch as I [Paul] am the apostle of the Gentiles, I magnify mine office. (Rom. 11:13)

Topic 4

The Holy Spirit's Teaching

The Holy Spirit teaches. The Holy Spirit will lead us to understanding. We must then follow Scripture and the instructions of Jesus to Paul. Paul has given us a model to follow throughout our lives. We are to be followers of Paul. Paul received the dispensation of grace from God who revealed to Paul the mystery of Christ. As members of the Body of Christ, we are to build upon the foundation established by Paul by doing good works. Our works will be judged good or bad and hopefully rewarded by God.

> Be ye followers of me [Paul], even as I also *am* of Christ. (1 Cor. 11:1; italics added)

> If ye have heard of the dispensation of the grace of God which is given me to you-ward:

> How that by revelation he made known unto me [Paul] the mystery; (as I wrote afore in few words),

Whereby, when ye read, ye may understand my [Paul] knowledge in the mystery of Christ)

Which in other ages was not made known unto the sons of men, as it is now revealed unto his holy apostles and prophets by the Spirit;

That the Gentiles should be fellow heirs, and of the same body, and partakers of his promise in Christ by the gospel:

Whereof I was made a minister, according to the gift of the grace of God given unto me by the effectual working of his power. (Eph. 3:2–7)

Topic 5

Works and Salvation

Works have no bearing on our salvation. However, we are to do good "works" as a member of the Body of Christ. These works are specifically for the Body of Christ and are taught by the apostle Paul. Christ is the cornerstone, and Paul is the wise master builder.

As we search the scriptures, the Holy Spirit will show us the truth. The truth of Scripture is found a little here and there. Scripture specifically states that man, having received the Holy Spirit of God, are to do good works. Paul is not talking about mowing lawns, cleaning yards, or painting houses (although this is commendable). We are talking about building up the Body of Christ. We are the ambassadors of Christ. The Body of Christ is stated only four times by Paul in the New Testament, yet the body has been being assembled (established) for almost two thousand years.

> According to the grace of God which is given unto me [Paul], as a wise master builder, I have laid the foundation, and another [you] buildeth thereon. But let every man take heed how he buildeth thereupon.
>
> For other foundation can no man lay than that is laid, which is Jesus Christ [cornerstone].

Now if any man [us] build upon this foundation gold, silver, precious stones, wood, hay, stubble;

Every man's work shall be made manifest [known]: for the day shall declare it, because it shall be revealed by fire; and the fire shall try every man's work of what sort it is.

If any man's work abide which he hath built thereupon, he shall receive a reward.

If any man's work shall be burned, he shall suffer loss: but he himself shall be saved; yet so as by fire. (1 Cor. 3:10–15)

Topic 6

Rapture and Tribulation

When the body is complete, Christ will then descend into the clouds and will call all who are dead in Christ and then those who live and remain. As we are now seated spiritually, we will then be seated in the heavenly realm. The scriptures shown below are not end-times events.

For if we believe that Jesus died and rose again, even so them also which sleep in Jesus will God bring with him.

For this we say unto you by the word of the Lord, that we which are alive *and* remain unto the coming of the Lord shall not prevent them which are asleep.

For the Lord himself shall descend from heaven with a shout, with the voice of the archangel, and with the trump of God: and the dead in Christ shall rise first:

Then we which are alive *and* remain shall be caught up together with them in the clouds, to meet the Lord in the air: and so shall we ever be with the Lord.

Wherefore comfort one another with these words. (1 Thess. 4:14–18; italics added)

Behold, I [Paul] shew you a mystery; We shall not all sleep, but we shall all be changed,

In a moment, in the twinkling of an eye, at the last trump: for the trumpet shall sound, and the dead shall be raised incorruptible, and we shall be changed. (1 Cor. 15:51–52)

Topic 7

Blessed Hope of Christ

We, the Body of Christ, shall be delivered from the wrath of the tribulation.

And to wait for his Son from heaven, whom he raised from the dead, *even* Jesus, which delivered us from the wrath to come. (1 Thess. 1:10; italics added)

Looking for that blessed hope, and the glorious appearing [Rapture], of the great God and our Saviour Jesus Christ. (Titus 2:13)

Topic 8

Spiritually Seated in Heavenly Places

Even though we are in the flesh, God and Jesus have provided a place for us (Body of Christ) as if we were with them now. This heavenly seating will take place at a future event. For now it is spiritual.

> And as we have borne the image of the earthy, we shall also bear the image of the heavenly. (1 Co. 15:49)

> Blessed *be* the God and Father of our Lord Jesus Christ, who hath blessed us with all spiritual blessings in heavenly *places* in Christ. (Eph. 1:3; italics added)

> And hath raised *us* up together, and made *us* sit together in heavenly *places* in Christ Jesus. (Eph. 2:6; italics added)

> For our conversation is in heaven; from whence also we look for the Saviour, the Lord Jesus Christ. (Phil. 3:20; italics added)

Topic 9

Under the Law and Ordinances

The commandments, laws, traditions, and ordinances of the Jews have all been nailed to the cross and were meant for the Jews. We, the Body of Christ, are under grace. The Law, ordinances, and such do not have anything to do with the Body of Christ (the church today) and are not required of us for salvation. Paul never stated that we should observe the Passover or any other ordinance or festival. He never observed these ordinances either. We are to walk after *in* the spirit.

> Having abolished in his flesh the enmity, *even* the law of commandments *contained* in ordinances; for to make in himself of twain one new man, *so* making peace. (Eph. 2:15; italics added)

> Blotting out the handwriting of ordinances that was against us, which was contrary to us, and took it out of the way, nailing it to his cross. (Col. 2:14)

Wherefore, my brethren, ye also are become dead to the law by the body of Christ; that ye should be married to another, *even* to him who is raised from the dead, that we should bring forth fruit [good works] unto God. (Rom. 7:4; italics added)

Know ye not that ye are the temple of God, and *that* the Spirit of God dwelleth in you? (1 Cor. 3:16; italics added)

In the day when God shall judge the secrets of men by Jesus Christ according to my [Paul's] gospel [1 Corinthians 15:1–4]. (Rom. 2:16)

Topic 10

Baptism and the Water Immersion Requirement

It is not necessary to confess your sins to the Holy Spirit or God for that matter. The Holy Spirit will remain in you and become part of you when you believed in the shed blood of Christ. You were baptized in the Holy Spirit.

When John baptized with water, the believers repented their sins but did not receive the blessing of the Holy Spirit. They were born again. We must remember that the book of Acts is a transitional book starting with Peter and the apostles and ending with the commission of the apostle Paul to the Gentiles. This is when the baptism issue changed from water to the Spirit of God.

> Then remembered I the word of the Lord, how that he said, *John indeed baptized with water; but ye shall be baptized with the Holy Ghost.* (Acts 11:16; italics added)

> For Christ sent me [Paul] not to baptize, but to preach the gospel: not with wisdom of words, lest the cross of Christ should be made of none effect. (1 Cor. 1:17)

Topic 11

Sin and Repentance

Nowhere in the books of Paul does he condemn us if we sin. Paul never tells us to repent. There are two types of sin: commissioned, meaning that which is planned and carried out; and noncommissioned, meaning our sin was not planned and happened by accident, usually without thinking. Scripture is very clear on this issue. Our sin, if any, has been *reconciled* by the shed blood of Christ. God has *justified* the Body of Christ. God is filled with goodness, *forbearance*, and long suffering.

> Likewise reckon ye also yourselves to be dead indeed unto sin, but alive unto God through Jesus Christ our Lord.
>
> Let not sin therefore reign in your mortal body, that ye should obey it in the lusts thereof.
>
> For sin shall not have *dominion* over you: for ye are not under the law, but under *grace*.
>
> What then? shall we sin, because we are not under the law, but under grace? God forbid.
>
> Being then made free from sin, ye became the servants of righteousness.
>
> But now being made free from sin, and become servants to God, ye have your

fruit unto holiness, and the end everlast-
ing life. (Rom. 6:11–18, 22; italics added)

But now we are delivered from the law,
that being dead wherein we were held;
that we should serve in newness of *spirit*,
and not *in* the oldness of the letter. (Rom.
7:6; italics added)

Wherefore henceforth know we no man
after the flesh: yea, though we have known
Christ after the flesh, yet now henceforth
know we *him* no more.

Therefore, if any man *be* in Christ,
he is a new creature: old things are passed
away; behold, all things are become new.

And all things *are* of God, who hath
reconciled us to himself by Jesus Christ,
and hath given to us the ministry of
reconciliation;

To wit, that God was in Christ, rec-
onciling the world unto himself, not
imputing their trespasses unto them;

and hath committed unto us the word of reconciliation.

Now then we are ambassadors for Christ, as though God did beseech *you* by us: we pray *you* in Christ's stead, be ye reconciled to God.

For he hath made him *to be* sin for us, who knew no sin; that we might be made the righteousness of God in him. (2 Cor. 5:16–21; italics added)

Reconciliation

"Reconciliation is the end of our estrangement to God, caused by original sin between God and humanity… Evangelical theologian Philip Ryken describes reconciliation in this way: '…God is the *author*, Christ is the *agent* and we are the *ambassadors* of reconciliation…'" (Wikipedia).

Justification

In Christian theology, justification is God's righteous act of removing the guilt and penalty of sin while, at the same time, declaring the ungodly to be righteous, through faith in Christ's atoning [blood] sacrifice (Wikipedia).

Whom God hath set forth *to be* a propitiation through faith in his blood, to declare his (Jesus) righteousness for the remission of *sins* that are past, through the *forbearance* of God. (Rom. 3:25; italics added)

Whosoever is born of God [not water baptism] doth not commit *sin*; for his seed (God) remaineth in him: and he cannot *sin*, because he is born of God. (1 John 3:9; italics added)

Forbearance

"'Forbearance' (anoche, 'a holding back') is ascribed to God (*Ro 2:4*, "the riches of his goodness and forbearance and longsuffering"; Ro 3:25 the Revised Version (Birtish and American), "*the passing over of the sins done aforetime, in the forbearance of God*," the King James Version 'remission' (margin 'passing over') of sins, that are past, through the forbearance of God") (W. L. Walker; italics added).

Topic 12

Shed Blood and the New Testament

Let me explain that the New Testament could only be enforced after Jesus died and was resurrected. Christ is the mediator of this covenant. The apostles new nothing of this. Even at Pentecost, Peter new nothing of the New Testament or the shed blood of Christ and its meaning. Jesus never explained to them, the apostles, the meaning of His shed blood.

> How much more shall the blood of Christ, who through the eternal Spirit offered himself without spot to God, purge your conscience from dead works to serve the living God?
>
> And for this cause he is the mediator of the new testament, that by means of death, for the redemption of the transgressions *that were* under the first testament, they which are called might receive the promise of eternal inheritance. (Heb. 9:14–15; italics added)

For this is my blood of the new testament, which is shed for many for the remission of sins. (Matt. 26:28)

And he said unto them, This is my blood of the new testament, which is shed for many. (Mark 14:24)

Likewise also the cup after supper, saying, This cup *is* the new testament in my blood, which is shed for you. (Luke 22:20; italics added)

Topic 13

Paul and Synagogues

Paul did not always go to synagogues, but he tried many times. He did during the first part of his ministry (in Acts) to preach Jesus Christ to the Jews and was almost killed for his efforts. But God maintained that he should go to the Gentiles.

But the Jews stirred up the devout and honorable women, and the chief men of the city, and raised persecution against Paul and Barnabas, and expelled them out of their coasts.

But they [Paul and Barnabas] shook off the dust of their feet against them [Jews], and came unto Iconium.

And the disciples were filled with joy, and with the Holy Ghost. (Acts 13:50–52)

And when Silas and Timotheus were come from Macedonia, Paul was pressed in the spirit, and testified to the Jews *that* Jesus *was* Christ.

And when they opposed themselves, and blasphemed, he [Paul] shook *his* raiment, and said unto them, Your blood *be* upon your own heads; I *am* clean: from henceforth I will go unto the Gentiles. (Acts 18:5–6; italics added)

And he [Jesus] said unto me [Paul], Depart: for I will send thee far hence unto the Gentiles. (Acts 22:21)

Delivering thee from the people [Jews], and from the Gentiles, unto whom now I [Jesus] send thee. (Acts 26:17)

Topic 14

Paul and the Jewish Law

"I [Paul] am verily a man *which am* a Jew, born in Tarsus, *a city* in Cilicia, yet brought up in this city at the feet of Gamaliel, *and* taught according to the perfect manner of the law of the fathers, and was zealous toward God, as ye [Jews] all are this day" (Acts 22:3; italics added).

Topic 15

Be Like Paul

"Be ye followers of me [Paul], even as I also *am* of Christ" (1 Cor. 11:1; italics added).

"Unto me [Paul], who am less than the least of all saints, is this grace given, that I should preach among the Gentiles the unsearchable riches of Christ" (Eph. 3:8).

Topic 16

Paul, Eternity, and Jesus

Yes, he is dead and is accounted worthy as one of those who followed Christ, yet his body is still in the grave. His spirit is with God, who gave it. There is a crown of righteousness waiting for him, but it will be given to him on that day. Paul will be given his reward on the day of Jesus Christ's return during the Rapture. Whatever we may face in this life—discouragement, persecution, or death—we know that our reward is with Christ in eternity.

> Then shall the dust [body] return to the earth as it was: and the spirit shall return unto God who gave it. (Eccles. 12:7)

> For I [Paul] am now ready to be offered, and the time of my departure is at hand.

> I have fought a good fight, I have finished *my* course, I have kept the faith:

> Henceforth there is laid up for me [Paul] a crown of righteousness, which the Lord, the righteous judge, shall give me at that day: and not to me only, but

unto all them also that love his appearing [Rapture]. (2 Tim. 4:6–8; italics added)

For I am in a strait betwixt two, having a desire to depart, and to be with Christ; which is far better. (Phil. 1:23)

Therefore, *we are* always confident, knowing that, whilst we are at home in the body, we are absent from the Lord:

(For we walk by faith, not by sight:)

We are confident, *I say*, and willing rather to be absent from the body, and to be present with the Lord. (2 Cor. 5:6–8; italics added)

SECTION 7

Armor of God

Be strong in prayer. Always be ready for an attack from the evil (devil) one. God will give us the strength to overcome his spiritual wickedness. Harden your faith so nothing or no one can shake it or cause you to doubt. Stand firm, and always be ready to overcome evil. Remember that God and Jesus know what we are going through, for Jesus had the same experiences. Be resolute in your faith.

> Finally, my brethren, be strong in the Lord, and in the power of his might.
>
> Put on the whole armour of God, that ye may be able to stand against the wiles of the devil.
>
> For we wrestle not against flesh and blood, but against principalities, against powers, against the rulers of the darkness

of this world, against spiritual wickedness in high *places.*

Wherefore take unto you the whole armour of God, that ye may be able to withstand in the evil day, and having done all, to stand.

Stand therefore, having your loins girt about with truth, and having on the breastplate of righteousness;

And your feet shod with the preparation of the gospel of peace;

Above all, taking the shield of faith, wherewith ye shall be able to quench all the fiery darts of the wicked.

And take the helmet of salvation, and the sword of the Spirit, which is the word of God:

Praying always with all prayer and supplication in the Spirit. (Eph. 6:10–18; italics added)

SECTION 8

A Letter from Christ Written on Human Hearts

> You show that you are a letter from Christ, the result of our ministry, written not with ink but with the Spirit of the living God, not on tablets of stone but on tablets of human hearts. (2 Cor. 3:3)

Let's break down and review the above passage for clarity.

> You [Body of Christ] show that you are a letter from Christ, the result of our [Paul and Timothy] ministry, written not with ink but with the Spirit of the living God, not on tablets of stone but on tablets of human hearts.

You—the Body of Christ.

Letter from Christ—this letter was admittedly from Christ himself, given to Paul through the Holy Spirit.

Result of our ministry—the spiritual work of Paul and Timothy and the dissemination of the truth of Christ's resurrection and our fulfillment in him.

Written not with ink—ink was temporary. The Ten Commandments were written by the finger of God. This letter was written by the very Spirit of the living God.

Tablets of stone and hearts—the Spirit's work in a person's life is far superior than rules written on stone. The heart is the seat of our emotions. It is obvious in this occasion that the hearts of the Body of Christ were moving spiritually.

The apostle Paul wrote this passage to the Corinthian church. The Corinthian church was founded by Paul on his second missionary journey. Many false apostles were going around to the saints in Corinth, discrediting the message of Paul and were peddling a different form of truth and salvation. Paul's authority was being challenged by these impostors. Paul wrote 2 Corinthians to reaffirm his credibility as an apostle and that all are seated with Christ as a member of the Body of Christ, and Christ is the head.

> Now ye are the body of Christ, and members in particular. (1 Cor. 12:27)

> And he is the head of the body, the church: who is the beginning, the firstborn from the dead; that in all *things* he might have the preeminence. (Col. 1:18)

WHEN STUDYING THE BIBLE, ALWAYS KEEP THIS IN MIND

The failure to rightly divide the Bible has turned it into a conglomeration of confusion. *Do not try to put together what God has separated.* According to the apostle Paul's teaching, God is dealing with different people through a different apostle and through a different gospel in a different way toward a different destination.

ABOUT THE AUTHOR

Cal and Christi Poulsen have
been married for forty-one years.
The love of their lives are five children; eleven grandchildren; and
their 103-pound German shepherd, Sammy 3. Early in their
marriage, they supported the fos-
ter care program in Racine, Wisconsin, having shared their
lives with fourteen foster children and participated in the
Crisis Intervention Program for troubled and endangered
youth.

God became an integral part of their lives in 1983,
providing love, guidance, and biblical teaching throughout the many churches they attended. Cal's personal background includes the nurturing of church administrations,
their members, and the youth.

They live in Round Lake, a sleepy little town near
the Fox River Chain O' Lakes in the northeast corner
of Illinois. Being retired, Cal has ample opportunity to

research Scripture and conduct Bible studies. He also loves to go bowling, reading, and fishing.

You may contact him at scriptureinsights@comcast.net.

CPSIA information can be obtained
at www.ICGtesting.com
Printed in the USA
LVHW112029150720
660524LV00014B/422